Superb Soups and Starters

The freshest fruits and vegetables form the basic
ingredients of this appetizing selection of wholefood
soups and starters – giving maximum nutrition,
colour and flavour. Includes a fruit and vegetable
seasonal guide.

By the same author

GLUTEN-FREE COOKING
RITA GREER'S EXTRAORDINARY KITCHEN
　NOTEBOOK
FOOD ALLERGY (with Dr Robert Woodward)
FRUIT AND VEGETABLES IN PARTICULAR
GLUTEN-FREE BUMPER BAKE BOOK
MANY SCARS
THE FIRST CLINICAL ECOLOGY COOKBOOK

Superb Soups and Starters

Easy to Make and Full of Goodness

by

Rita Greer

THORSONS PUBLISHERS LIMITED
Wellingborough, Northamptonshire

First published 1981

British Library Cataloguing in Publication Data

Greer, Rita
  Superb soups and starters.
  1. Soups
  2. Cookery (Appetizers)
  I. Title
  641.8'13   TX757

  ISBN 0-7225-0691-0

Photoset by
Specialised Offset Services Ltd., Liverpool.
Printed in Great Britain by
The Thetford Press, Thetford, Norfolk,
and bound by Weatherby Woolnough,
Wellingborough, Northamptonshire.

Contents

Introduction

This book features food to promote *health*. The recipes are simple and are built around fresh ingredients, which naturally relate to the seasons of the year. We live in times when over-rich, undernourishing, all-season junk foods are the norm in the West. These do not feature in this book!

Good food requires good, fresh ingredients. Any recipe which starts, 'a teaspoonful of dried onion flakes', or 'one packet of frozen ...', or 'open a tin of ...' is doomed to failure, and deserves to vanish without trace ... So recipes in this book call for fresh (not frozen or tinned) vegetables and fruit *in season*.

This provides a subtle, psychological link with the natural resources of the earth, and ensures the very best results. (Many people nowadays have no awareness of the natural rhythm of the seasons – they eat strawberries at Christmas and sprouts in June, thanks to the use of freezers.) As for tinned vegetables, what poor relations they are of the fresh vegetable – overcooked, swimming about in water, artificially coloured and even artificially flavoured too in some cases. Any vitamins and minerals are left in more by accident than by design! Such foods may be convenient, but this is at the expense of most other characteristics associated with food.

Leaving the junk/convenience/carnivore recipes to others I hope you will read on to learn about soups and starters which will give you maximum nutrition, flavour, colour and variety.

Just to remind you of the wonderful harvest of vegetables and fruit available to you, here is a brief guide to their seasons and variety.

Seasonal Vegetable Guide

Vegetables may become available earlier or later depending on whether spring is early or late and the type of weather during the growing seasons.

January   Cabbages, sprouts, kale, cauliflower, celery, leeks, parsnips, swede.

February   Broccoli, leeks, parsnips, celery, sprouts, swedes, cauliflower.

March   Last of sprouts, first of spinach, broccoli, leeks, parsnips, swedes, cauliflower.

April   Lettuces, radishes, salad onions, last of leeks, parsnips, spinach, cabbages, cauliflower.

May   Usually the worst month of the year for vegetables – broccoli, cabbages, spinach, lettuces, radishes, spring onions, early courgettes – shortages are common.

June   Things improve considerably this month – broad beans, peas, new potatoes, cabbages, cauliflower, spinach, lettuce, tomatoes, radishes, cucumbers, courgettes.

July   French and runner beans, broad beans, peas, cucumbers, courgettes, marrows, calabrese, cauliflowers, spinach, new carrots and turnips, new beetroot, new potatoes, tomatoes.

August   French beans, runner beans, broad beans, last of peas, calabrese, cauliflowers, cabbages, new carrots, turnips, new potatoes, cucumbers, beetroot, tomatoes.

September   French beans, runner beans, second-crop broad beans and peas, marrows, ridge cucumbers, cauliflowers, cabbages, new sprouts, celery, tomatoes.

October   Cauliflower, cabbage, beetroot, sprouts, new swedes.

November   Celery, leeks, parsnips, cabbage, sprouts, turnips, beetroot.

December   Celery, leeks, parsnips, cabbages, sprouts, spinach, broccoli.

Some vegetables are available all year round because they can be stored. Others are grown commercially and command a high price, being out of season most of the year. Some are imported from overseas, where the seasons are not the same as ours.

Available all the year round – cress, mushrooms, carrots, onions, green peppers, cucumbers, tomatoes, potatoes, garlic.

Available on and off all year round – watercress, celery, beansprouts, beetroot.

It is quite amazing how many people buy fresh fruit and vegetables and then do not use them for days. Buy little and often so as not to fall into that trap if you can. Although the general standard of vegetables is high and the variety good, supermarkets are not the only place to shop. A good, small greengrocers shop is a wonderful asset to any cook. Fortunately, there are plenty of them about. They are best for very basic vegetables and fruit. More exotic items will have to be bought from supermarkets or health food stores.

Store perishable items in the fridge and use as soon as possible. Not-so-perishable items, such as root vegetables, should be kept in a cool dry, well-ventilated place.

Fruits in Season

Fruit seasons are a little more complicated. Some fruits have only a very short season – sometimes only a few days – and harvesting time depends very much on what kind of spring (late or early) we have and how quickly the fruit ripens. A good deal of fruit is grown abroad and imported to meet demand and this usually arrives in the shops before our own season starts.

In very general terms, the following are available at sometime during the months of June, July and August – peaches, strawberries, cherries, apricots, plums, raspberries, greengages, gooseberries, blackberries, blackcurrants, redcurrants, figs, pomegranates, nectarines.

These are available all the year round – oranges, grapefruit, bananas, apples, pears, cooking apples.

Melons, pineapples and grapes are available on and off all the year round. Other members of the citrus fruit family enjoy a short season around Christmas – tangerines, satsumas, etc.

Nuts can be stored and used as required, so these too are available all the year round. The freshest tasting nuts are shelled just before use.

The Kitchen

Once I had got the message that gadgets do not necessarily increase one's skill, I became a much better cook. Only basic tools are needed – skill comes with practice. Attitude of mind is of great importance. Aim at a high standard for simple food and it is hard to go wrong. Complicated recipes, although more trouble to prepare, do not always produce the best food.

I hope you will find the recipes in this book very easy and quick to prepare. The basic kitchen equipment needed covers only a small range as you will see.

1. *Vegetable knife.* A light, strong knife, shaped to a point with a comfortable wooden handle that will not slip. Keep it sharp always and have respect for it. Cut away from your fingers at a slight angle, never towards them. (No, you do not need a set of twelve assorted cook's knives – a vegetable knife and one other larger one will do.)

2. *Chopping board.* Use the vegetable knife with a wooden chopping board. A largish board is best. (I confess to using an old pastry board myself.)

3. *Soup ladle.* There is no substitute for a soup ladle, which is really only a cup on a long handle.

4. *Blender.* People who do not have one of these imagine that they are fearfully expensive. Well, some on the market are, but some of the cheapest makes are, in fact, the best. One speed is all that is needed. Buy one with the on/off switch at the side so it cannot be knocked accidentally. (I still have painful memories of one

model I had with a large switch right in the front. I accidentally switched it on *before* I had put the lid on but *after* I had filled the goblet with hot leeks and stock. The mess was beyond description, as was the cook.)
Golden rules for using a blender:
—— Always make sure the actual blender is switched *off*

before plugging it in to the main electricity supply.

—— Always check the lid is really secure before activating.

—— Do not overfill.

—— Do not put liquids which are too hot into the goblet.

—— Always rinse the goblet with water immediately after use.

—— Be careful not to switch on by accident before you are ready to blend.

—— Keep the machine clean.

5. *Sieve.* Just occasionally you will need to strain a soup. Buy a fine metal mesh one, not a plastic one. It should be a fairly large one. Rinse upside down under the water tap immediately after use, to wash out strainings caught in the mesh.

6. *Wooden spoon.* An essential for stirring and mixing.

7. *Saucepans.* Aluminium pans tend to get pitted. Enamelled ones can discolour. Cast iron pans need a

very strong arm when full. Stainless steel pans are lightest to handle, strong and easy to keep shining and clean. Whichever sort you have, well-fitting lids are essential. A frying pan with reasonably high sides is an important utensil too. If intending to use cream, a very small saucepan just for heating it is very useful. You would probably have to go to a kitchen (specialist) shop for one.

8. *Rolling pin*. Just a plain pine one will do. No need to have a hollow one to fill with iced water or one that rotates. (I know good cooks who use an ordinary bottle with excellent results!)

9. *Bowls and basins*. Any kind will do. Strongest and most chip-proof are the glass ones. Small, medium and large are all you need.

10. *Baking sheet*. No need to buy a non-stick one – just get one that fits your oven shelves. They are handy for both baking on directly and for putting other baking containers on just to get an even heat.

11. *Quiche dish*. There are many types on the market. Some people swear by metal ones, but a glass ovenproof or a pottery one placed on a baking sheet will do nicely.

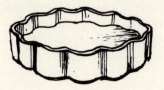

12. *Colander*. Get one with plenty of holes in, preferably a metal or enamel one. The kind with a long handle is easiest to use.

13. *Egg whisk*. A small wire hand whisk (as illustrated) will do.

14. *Grapefruit knife*. This is a curved, serrated-edged knife specially designed for loosening grapefruit segments.

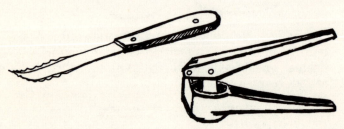

15. *Garlic press*. Choose a strong metal one, not a plastic one.

16. *Pestle and mortar.* Buy a hefty one as pounding into it requires much strength!

17. *Citrus juicer.* One of the old-fashioned hand ones is quite effective. The kind with a dish underneath to catch the juice is a good idea, but do not buy it if you think the actual extractor does not have enough edges to do the job properly. Most efficient of all are the electric ones which turn while you hold the fruit. Some blender motors have a juicer attachment, or you can buy a citrus juicer on its own.

18. *Cherry stoner.* Sometimes this comes with the garlic press, half way up the handle.

Cooking Terms Explained

Fry. This is always done in oil or fat of some kind such as margarine. Heat the oil or fat and then put in the vegetable – usually onion – lower the heat so that it cooks gently. Stir now and then to make the cooking even.

Bring to the boil. Use a fairly fast heat (unless the recipe tells you otherwise). When bubbles begin to appear, give a stir and turn down the heat or remove pan if you are using electric.

Boil. This is a continuous process over a high heat to make a constant bubbling. It is rarely used in cooking. A most destructive way of preparing food.

Simmer. This is a lazy kind of action. Use a level of heat which will keep the food at a constant temperature while it cooks. It bears no relation to boiling. Look for slight ripples, not bubbles.

Chop. Do this on a board with a large knife. Keep fingers well away from the cutting edge. Cut away from you, making small pieces of vegetable (cubes/dice).

Slice. Hold the vegetable firmly with one hand, slice with a small sharp knife, away from you, on a chopping board.

Stir. Use a wooden spoon. Move it around the saucepan right through the vegetables and slide it round the edge of the pan. This action both mixes and loosens food.

Blend or liquidize. See previous section on equipment for details. Gives you a *purée*.

Strain. This is a way of separating out lumps and fibre from the main body of a soup. Put the sieve over a saucepan or bowl and pour in the soup. Some liquid will pass through immediately. Use the back of a wooden spoon, pressing the mush that forms in the sieve to squeeze out more liquid. Discard mush.

Chill. This is not the same as 'freeze'. It merely means to cool at fridge (not freezer) temperature.

Planning a Meal

1. Try to achieve a nutritional balance. Is there enough protein? Is there too much fat? Is there enough roughage? Is there too much carbohydrate?
2. Make a meal with a *variety* of textures and colours.

3. Arrange the vegetarian meal to give you basically:
   —— At least two kinds of protein from nuts, cheese, eggs, milk and pulses.
   —— No more than two kinds of starches from potatoes, rice, pasta and wholewheat grains.
   —— Several kinds of vegetables and fruit for vitamins, minerals, fibre and variety of colour and texture.
   —— A small amount of fat from thin cooking oil.
4. Start with one course and build the rest of the meal around that, e.g. cauliflower cheese – this has quite a bit of fat in it (as well as protein), so the other two courses can be relatively low in fat. There is not a lot of starch in this main course so you could afford to do fruit-filled pancakes and a soup with either potato or pasta in it. Cauliflower cheese is very pale coloured so your soup could be bright and have more than one vegetable (I would choose a vegetable soup). So let's look at the full menu:

   Mixed vegetable soup (including potato)
   Cauliflower cheese
   Fruit filled pancakes
5. Think of the meal as a whole and not as a separate list of items. You will then avoid such blunders as cheese soup, cauliflower cheese and cheesecake to follow or, quiche, omelette, and lemon meringue pie!
6. Remember, everybody is delighted with simple foods if they are cooked to perfection (or left raw) and served attractively. Do not choose to make more than one complicated course out of three – people will not expect it.

Presentation

Regarding the presentation of food (or how you serve it), make sure your crockery and cutlery are spotless, as should be the table linen, mats, etc. Hot items should be served on hot plates, cold items on cold plates. Plates and bowls should be a generous size for the portions served on them. Dishing out is an art in itself. Use a ladle for soup or pour from a jug. Serve vegetables with a spoon and fork and place them neatly on the plates.

Soups

1
General Advice

Soup served at the start of a meal should be stimulating to the appetite, paving the way for other quite different food. In no way should it make you feel 'full up', so you should not serve too much. One average soup ladle plus a little more satisfies most people. When serving hot soup, make sure the soup bowls or plates are hot too.

The majority of soup recipes start with 'fry the onion in the oil'. Choose firm, medium or small onions. (Larger varieties are usually too mild in flavour.) Cut off the top and bottom of the onion, peel away the papery skin and slice finely for best results. If you fry chunks then the onion flavour is likely to be too strong when only the outside of each chunk is cooked and not the inside. It is a good idea to agitate the onion a little during frying. Use a wooden spoon for this, the main object being to lightly cook the onion to a transparent state *without letting it brown*.

Always use a good-sized saucepan with a strong handle and a lid, so that when you add cold water etc. to a hot pan, this will avoid splashes and overfilling.

Any fool can make a soup? Not so! The actual business of seasoning can be difficult. Taste first and then, a little at a time, put in your salt, freshly-ground black pepper, sugar, etc. Keep tasting and adding until it is right. Be on the mean side rather than the generous – a pinch at a time (stirred in well) to avoid disaster. Aim at bringing the flavour out of a soup, rounding it off and making it a 'complete' taste. This is an art, not a science, and exact amounts of seasoning vary from soup to soup. When you taste, you should evaluate *immediate taste, taste while swallowing* and *after-taste*. These three stages should satisfy, but tempt you to take more. Adjust seasoning when the soup is the same temperature at which it is to be served. In other words, if serving a soup hot, season it while hot.

Stock for Soups

Every hot soup needs some body in the form of *stock*. As this is a vegetarian cookbook, ordinary beef or chicken stock cubes are out of the question. My own favourite stock is thin (not thickened) soy sauce, such as *La Choy* or *Amoy*. This is made principally from soya beans and so is vegetarian. Other people may prefer to use yeast extract such as *Barmene* or *Marmite*. The drawback with these is their saltiness. If you use yeast extract, make sure you do not use too much and take the salt into consideration when seasoning the soup. (Most grocers, supermarkets and health food stores in the U.K. sell soy sauce.)

There are vegetarian stock cubes available, but they are expensive as a rule and usually have far too many additives such as monosodium glutamate.

Two other items can be considered useful to add to the stock in a soup. One is tomato *purée* and the other is tinned Italian tomatoes. Neither of them taste like fresh tomatoes, but their very character, bright red colour and slightly sweet taste, can sometimes lift a dull soup up to an interesting level by enriching the stock. Tubes of *purée* are the most useful. Both items are made from just tomatoes and salt-water, which is a comfort now that chemical additives are so common in purchased food.

Enriching Soups

There is no doubt about it, cream added to soups rounds off their flavour, gives them a good texture and makes them rich. Unfortunately, it also adds cholesterol in the form of animal fat and a lot of unnecessary calories.

Personally, I hardly ever use cream in soups. A creamy effect can be obtained with the addition of potato while in the cooking stage. There is a strong move away from over-rich fatty foods in the enlightened health conscious diet. (You will find cream mentioned very rarely in these recipes.) However, should you wish to add it, remember it must be added hot to hot soup or it will curdle, i.e. both the cream and the soup should be about the same temperature. If you wish to add milk, the rule is the same – add hot milk to hot soup.

Thickening for Soups

The soups in this book vary in thickness, and if you wish to thicken soup use maize flour. This will alter the texture but not the flavour.

Take one level tablespoonful of maize flour and put it in a cup. Add two tablespoonsful water and stir to a smooth cream. Add two tablespoonsful of your soup and stir well. Pour into the soup, which should be hot. Bring to the boil and stir while simmering for about two to three minutes. The soup will gradually thicken. For a slightly thinner soup, put in just two level teaspoonsful of maize flour.

Soups: Past and Present

The role of soup both in our diet and in our culinary economics has changed since the arrival of the blender as a kitchen gadget. The 'waste not want not' attitude which prevailed in the Victorian household meant that most of the meat bones, meat and fish scraps and vegetable leftovers went into the constantly simmering stockpot. The rich stocks that emerged were used for gravies and sauces as well as the basis for soups. Nowadays who would have enough bones and leftovers to make such a stock? I am quite sure most of us would not fancy a large saucepan of bones and leftovers simmering all day on our stoves. I know I wouldn't!

Some of the 'waste not want not' attitude remains in that most people save the water that vegetables have been cooked in as a stock addition. (Better to put it into gravy or soup than waste it by throwing it down the drain.)

Where the modern blender-type soup differs too much from our great grandmothers' stockpot-soups is that stock has become of secondary importance and the flavour and goodness of the vegetable which forms the basis of the modern soup is now of primary importance. Mere flavour and kitchen economy has made way for nutrition and variation. This is why I do not advocate reheating and blending a nondescript pile of leftovers and calling it 'soup'. It is not soup in the modern sense – it is really liquidized leftovers with minimum flavour and even less value nutritionally speaking. (I call this 'dustbin soup'!)

Always use the best vegetables available and the freshest. Green things which have started to turn yellow and wilt are a waste of money even if their price looks like a bargain. (You can only make Wilting Lettuce Soup from wilting lettuce!) If you buy fresh vegetables in season all the year round you can *always* find something at a few pence per pound to use for soup.

Herbs and Seasonings for Soups

Fresh Parsley. This is useful as a garnish in sprigs and

chopped as a sprinkle. Greengrocers sell it fresh; some supermarkets do too. It can be grown in the garden or in a windowsill pot. If faint-hearted, buy a root or two from a garden shop for good results. Some people advocate growing from seed, after pouring a kettle of hot water over the area for sowing. Mature plants obligingly grow new shoots if you keep cutting sprigs off. Dried parsley cannot compare with fresh and is a poor substitute.

Chives. These too can be grown in the garden or in a window sill pot. Snip off as required. They are easier to grow than parsley and their mild oniony flavour always tastes fresh. Either chop with a knife, on a board, or snip with kitchen scissors. Dried chives are but a poor substitute for fresh.

Salt. For the clearest, sharpest taste, use sea salt crystals. These are sold in supermarkets and health food stores. Do not over-salt – health conscious people are taking much less these days. If you want to use a substitute try *Ruthmol* which is a potassium salt. Available from chemists.

Pepper. The best pepper for cooking is freshly ground peppercorns. Use a grinder and whole black peppercorns. Buy at the grocers or supermarket.

Self-raising Flour

You can make your own self-raising flour by adding baking powder to plain wholewheat flour (follow instructions on the tin). Once you have made up a quantity put it into a container and label it.

Accompaniments to Soup

Sippets or Croûtons

Cut thick slices of wholemeal bread. Trim off crusts and
discard. Cut what remains into cubes. Fry in hot oil,
turning them over to brown on all sides. Serve hot,
sprinkled into soup. Allow half a slice of bread per
person.

Brown Rice

Follow directions on the packet. Sprinkle one level
teaspoonful *cooked* rice per person into soup and heat
through. Rice is mostly used for thin soups or broths, just
to make them a little more filling.

Cheese Straws

**4 oz (100g) 100 per cent wholewheat flour or
wholewheat self-raising flour
or use 2 oz (50g) of each
small sprinkle of cayenne pepper
2 oz (50g) soft margarine
1 egg yolk
2 oz (50g) cheddar cheese, finely grated
1 tablespoonful water**

Preheat oven 425°-450°F/218°-232°C (Gas Mark 7). Mix flour and pepper together in a large bowl. Rub in the margarine until mixture resembles fine bread-crumbs. Stir in the grated cheese. Bind with egg yolk and water. Knead into a firm dough. Roll out using more flour and cut into $\frac{1}{4}$ inch wide $2\frac{1}{2}$ inch long fingers. Bake near the top of the oven for seven to ten minutes. Leave to cool on the tin. Serve warm or cold.

Pancake Strips

These are sometimes quicker to make than noodles. To make enough for four you will need:

**1 egg, beaten
1 pinch freshly grated nutmeg
2 oz (50g) 100 per cent wholewheat flour
6 tablespoonsful water
very small bunch of fresh chives, chopped
1 tablespoonful cooking oil**

Put the egg and nutmeg into a mixing bowl. Alternately stir in flour and water. Use a wooden spoon to thoroughly mix after each addition. This will ensure that there are no lumps. When all the flour and water are mixed in, sprinkle in the chives. Heat half the oil in a frying pan, tipping it to make sure the pan is well oiled. (The pan needs to be hot enough for a faint haze to rise off the oil.) Pour half the batter into the pan. Tip it all ways to spread the batter evenly. Cook on both sides until golden and slightly transparent. Keep the pancake warm while you cook the second. Put one on top of the other and cut into thin strips. Put these into hot clear soups.

Wholewheat Pasta/Noodles

It is worth going to a specialist shop for these, where you will find a good variety, both for shape and colour. Choose small types for soup. Follow the instructions on the packet. (Put into soups when cooked.) Always good in soups that are made with tomato. Use to make a thin soup more filling and more interesting – just a sprinkle is all you need.

Garlic Spread

4 oz (100g) soft margarine
1 tablespoonful finely chopped (washed) parsley
1 clove garlic, peeled and put
through a garlic press

Put all ingredients into a bowl and mix well. Use to spread on bread which has been crisped in a fairly hot oven for ten minutes or on wholewheat toast.

Food Bread

12 oz (300g) wholewheat flour
2 oz (50g) wheatgerm
1 oz (25g) bran
1 level teaspoon salt
½ pint (300ml) lukewarm water
¼ oz (7g) dried yeast
2 generous teaspoonsful runny honey
2 tablespoonsful cold water
½ oz (15g) dried milk granules
1 egg

Put the flour, wheatgerm, bran and salt into a warm basin. Mix with a spoon to distribute evenly. Measure out ½ pint lukewarm water in a small basin, sprinkle in the yeast and dribble in the honey. Leave for five minutes.

Use a basin to mix the 2 tablespoonsful of cold water with the dried milk. Beat in the eggs with a fork until you have a thin liquid. Put to one side.

When the yeast has softened mix to dissolve into the liquid. Make a well in the centre of the flour and pour in the yeast/honey/water mixture. Leave for 5-10 minutes until bubbles form on the top. Now pour in the milk/egg mixture and with a wooden spoon mix to form a soft dough. Add a little more wholewheat flour and knead with the hands for about a minute, into a round shape. Put this back into the bowl and cover with a clean tea-towel. Leave to rise (prove) in a warm place.

When nearly double in size, turn out on to a floured worktop and knead for a minute. Shape into a long oval loaf and put on to an oiled baking sheet.

Leave to rise again, covered with the tea-towel. When it looks nice and plump and has risen almost double put into a pre-heated oven 400°F/200°C (Gas Mark 6) for ½ hour middle shelf. Turn down the heat to 350°F/180°C (Gas Mark 4) and bake for a further 10 minutes. When brown and crusty and smelling gorgeous, put on to a wire rack to cool.

Note. This bread is more nutritious than just plain wholewheat bread. The egg, wheatgerm and milk give it a much higher protein value.

Iron Rations Loaf

This is a rather unusual bread, a dark ginger colour and with a good taste. It is not as sweet as one would imagine with such a large amount of treacle. Higher in iron than ordinary bread, it only needs one proving so is quite quick to make.

½ pint (300ml) lukewarm water
¼ oz (7g) dried yeast granules
2 tablespoonsful black treacle
12 oz (350g) wholewheat flour
1 tablespoonful sunflower oil (or similar)
1 teaspoonful salt

Measure the water into a jug and sprinkle in the yeast granules. Leave to soften (about 4-5 minutes).

Gently warm (note 'warm') the black treacle to make it into a thin liquid. Add to the yeast and water and leave for 5 minutes. Stir well.

Mix the flour, oil and salt in a bowl and pour in the liquid. Mix with a wooden spoon to a stiff paste. Turn out on to a floured worktop and knead, using more flour. Shape into a round loaf and put on to a greased (use oil) baking sheet. Leave to rise in a warm place, covered with a clean cloth. When about doubled in size, put into a pre-heated oven 375°F/190°C (Gas Mark 5) and bake, middle shelf, for about 1 hour. Put on to a wire rack to cool.

2
Hot Soups

French Onion Soup
(Serves 4)

2 large onions – about 1 lb (450g)
1 oz (25g) margarine
1 tablespoonful 100 per cent wholewheat flour
1¼ pints (850ml) water
1 tablespoonful thin soy sauce
½ teaspoonful tomato *purée*
4 slices wholewheat bread
4 oz (100g) grated Gruyère cheese

Peel the onions and chop them finely. Melt the margarine in a saucepan and put in the onion. Do not let them brown, but cook until transparent, stirring frequently. Sprinkle in the flour and stir well with a wooden spoon. Cook like this for about a minute. Gradually pour in the water and soy sauce. Add the tomato *purée*. Stir well, bring to the boil, then lower heat and simmer (with the lid on) for about half an hour. Season to taste. Serve hot with toasted slices of wholemeal bread cut into cubes and cheese sprinkled into the hot soup.

Follow by a light main meal, such as a salad and a substantial pudding. If preferred, serve with toasted wholewheat bread with cheese, grilled and cut into fingers.

Filling. Creamy-brown in colour. Serve hot.

Onion and Potato Soup
(Serves 3)

This is an all-the-year-round soup as both potatoes and onions can be stored and used as required.

**1 large onion (or 2 medium), peeled and sliced
thinly
1 tablespoonful sunflower oil
1 clove garlic, peeled and chopped
2 medium potatoes, peeled and sliced
¾ pint (425ml) water, cold
2 teaspoonful soy sauce
Sea salt and freshly ground black pepper**

Fry the onion in the oil for two to three minutes with the garlic. Stir all the time with a wooden spoon. Put in the potato, soy sauce and about half the water. Heat through, put on the lid and simmer for about ten minutes until the potato is tender. Remove from heat. Add the rest of the water and liquidize. Pour back into the saucepan and season to taste. Serve hot after another three to five minutes simmering.

Very filling. Creamy beige in colour. Serve hot.

Split Pea Soup

(Serves 4-5)

A very substantial start to a meal.

**½ lb (225g) split peas
1 large onion, peeled and sliced
1 oz (25g) margarine
1 pint (550ml) water
1 tablespoonful soy sauce
½ lb (225g) carrots, trimmed, scrubbed and sliced
Sea salt and freshly ground black pepper**

Wash the split peas, under the cold tap, in a fine wire sieve. Put into a large bowl with at least 1¼ pints (700ml) cold water. Leave overnight to swell. Fry the onion in the margarine for three to four minutes. Pour in the pint (550ml) of water and the soy sauce. Strain the split peas (if necessary) and add to the saucepan with the carrots and a little salt. Bring to the boil and simmer gently, with the lid on for 1-1¼ hours. Stir from time to time. If the soup thickens too much, add more water. Season to taste. For a smoother soup, allow to cool and then liquidize.

Follow with a salad course and also a light fruit sweet. This soup can be served all the year round, but is traditionally for the cold winter months.

Very filling. Golden in colour. Serve hot.

Cheese Soup
(Serves 2-3)

1 small onion, peeled and thinly sliced
2 heaped teaspoonsful margarine
1 level teaspoonful maize flour
½ pint (275ml) skimmed milk
½ pint (275ml) cold water
1 teaspoonful soy sauce
Freshly ground black pepper
3 oz (75g) grated cheddar cheese

Fry the onion in the margarine for a few minutes. Mix the maize flour with a tablespoonful of the cold water. Stir into the rest of the water. Add both this, the ½ pint (275ml) milk and the soy sauce to the cooked onion. Bring to the boil and then simmer for about three minutes while stirring. Continue stirring while you sprinkle in the cheese. DO NOT BOIL! This will ruin the soup. Stir until melted. Serve at once, with sippets. If you think it does not taste cheesy enough, sprinkle a little grated cheese on the top and serve.

Very filling. Creamy-yellow in colour. Serve hot.

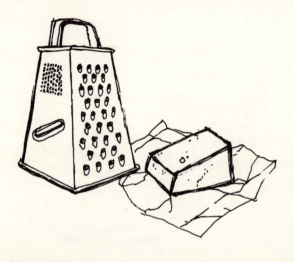

Lentil Soup
(Serves 4)

A very thick substantial soup available all the year round.

5 oz (150g) lentils
2 medium onions
1 medium potato, peeled and sliced thinly
2 tablespoonsful thin cooking oil
1 tablespoonful soy sauce
1 pint (550ml) water
Sea salt and freshly ground black pepper

Wash the lentils in a wire sieve. Soak overnight in a large bowl with about 1 pint (550ml) water. Fry the onion in the oil, using a large pan. Add the soy sauce, the strained lentils, the water and a little salt. Bring to the boil and simmer for about 40 minutes. Remove from heat, allow to cool and liquidize for a smooth creamy soup. (Omit this last stage if desired.) Reheat to serve.

Very filling. Apricot in colour. Serve hot.

Leek and Potato Soup
(Serves 4)

A smooth creamy soup, pale green and very satisfying.
1 medium onion
1 tablespoonful thin cooking oil
2 medium-sized leeks, trimmed of the coarsest green
and roots, sliced lengthwise, washed thoroughly, cut
into pieces
2 medium-sized potatoes, peeled and sliced
¾ pint (425ml) water
2 teaspoonsful soy sauce
Sea salt and freshly ground black pepper

Fry the onion in the oil. Add the leeks, potatoes and about half the water. Bring to the boil and simmer gently for about ten to fifteen minutes, with the lid on. Add the rest of the water to cool the soup down. Liquidize and return to saucepan. Taste, season and serve.

Very filling. Creamy-green in colour. Serve hot.

Minestrone Soup
(Serves 4-6)

Count this as a main meal as it is high in protein. Follow with a light salad and then a fruit-based sweet.

**3 oz (75g) haricot beans
1½ pints (850ml) water
2 medium onions, peeled and sliced thinly
2 tablespoonsful thin cooking oil
1 clove garlic, peeled and crushed
1 stick celery, trimmed, washed and chopped finely
1 medium carrot, washed, trimmed and finely diced
3 medium tomatoes, skinned and chopped
1 tablespoonful thin soy sauce
⅛ of a medium-sized cabbage, washed and finely
shredded
2 oz (50g) wholewheat pasta broken into short lengths
2 heaped tablespoonsful freshly chopped, washed
parsley
grated Parmesan cheese**

Put the beans to swell overnight in the water. The next day, fry the onion in the oil for two to three minutes, with the garlic. Put in the soaked beans and the water in which they were soaked. Put a lid on the pan and bring to the boil. Simmer gently with the lid on for about 1¼ hours. Add the celery, carrot, soy sauce, tomatoes, cabbage and pasta. Bring to the boil again adding a little more water if you think it necessary. Season lightly and simmer for about 30 minutes with the lid on. Taste and season. Serve hot, sprinkled with the parsley and cheese. Tinned tomatoes can be used instead of fresh.

Very substantial, very filling. Reddish-brown in colour.
Serve hot.

Potato Soup
(Serves 4)

This is the king of filling soups, to be followed by a main course that is very light (low starch) and an even lighter sweet. Serve all year round; most popular during the cold winter months. Choose potatoes that have a good flavour such as King Edwards. The tomato *purée* will colour it a delicate pink.

1 medium onion, peeled and sliced thinly
1 tablespoonful thin cooking oil
3 medium potatoes, peeled and sliced thinly
1½ pints (850ml) water
1 tablespoonful thin soy sauce
1 heaped teaspoonful tomato *purée*
1 heaped teaspoonful finely chopped (washed) fresh parsley
Sea salt and freshly ground black pepper

Fry the onion in the oil for three to four minutes. Add the potato slices, about a pint (550ml) of the water, the soy sauce and the tomato *purée*. Bring to the boil and simmer with the lid on for 15-25 minutes, depending on the age and variety of the potatoes. Remove from heat. Add the rest of the water and liquidize. Pour back into the saucepan. Stir in the parsley. Taste and season.

Very filling. Pale pink in colour. Serve hot.

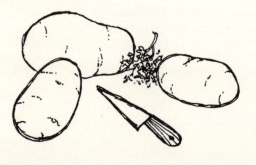

Parsnip Soup

(Serves 4)

A lovely creamy soup, full of flavour and slightly sweet.

1 medium onion, peeled and sliced thinly
1 tablespoonful thin cooking oil
¾ lb (350g) prepared parsnip, cut into small cubes
½ stick celery, washed and sliced
1½ pints (850ml) water
2 teaspoonsful soy sauce
Sea salt and freshly ground black pepper
1 level teaspoonful freshly chopped parsley

Use a large saucepan to fry the onion in the oil for a few minutes. Add the parsnip, celery, about two-thirds of the water and the soy sauce. Bring to the boil and simmer for about 15 minutes, with the lid on. Remove from heat and add the rest of the water. Blend and return to saucepan. Taste. Season and add the parsley. Heat and serve. If it turns out too sweet, add two or three drops fresh lemon juice.

Filling. Cream in colour. Serve hot.

French Country Soup
(Serves 4-5)

This hot soup has no onion in it, as the leeks serve as a base.

1 lb (450g) leeks, trimmed, sliced lengthways, washed thoroughly and sliced finely
3 carrots, washed, trimmed and chopped into small pieces
1½ tablespoonsful thin cooking oil
1 lb (450g) potatoes, peeled and sliced thinly
1½ pints (850ml) water, or a little over
1 tablespoonful thin soy sauce
Sea salt and freshly ground black pepper
1 tablespoonful finely chopped (washed) parsley

Fry the leeks and the carrots in the oil, while stirring for three to four minutes. Add the potato slices, just over a pint (550ml) of the water and then the soy sauce. Bring to the boil and simmer with the lid on for about 20-25 minutes. Remove from heat. Add the rest of the water and liquidize. Return to saucepan. Taste and season. Reheat and stir in parsley.

Very filling. Sandy colour. Serve hot.

Broad Bean Soup
(Serves 3-4)

This sounds a dreadfully dull soup but, in fact, it is an unusual flavour and a lovely sage green colour.

1 medium onion, peeled and sliced thinly
1 tablespoonful thin cooking oil
8 oz (225g) shelled broad beans (225g) – about 1¼ lb
(550g) in the pod will give you these
1 tablespoonful thin soy sauce
1 pint (550ml) water
Sea salt and freshly ground black pepper
little sugar

Fry the onion in the oil for three to four minutes. Add the broad beans, soy sauce and about two-thirds of the water. Bring to the boil. Simmer with the lid on for 15 minutes if the beans are small; 20 minutes if they are on the larger side. Remove from heat. Add the rest of the water and liquidize. Return to saucepan. Taste. Season with salt and pepper and if a bit too 'mineral' in taste, rectify with a few pinches sugar (keep tasting). Serve hot with *croûtons* or just as it is.

Whenever I make this soup I never fail to marvel at its creamy consistency – rather like fresh pea soup. Broad bean fans will be ecstatic.

Filling. Sage green in colour. Serve hot.

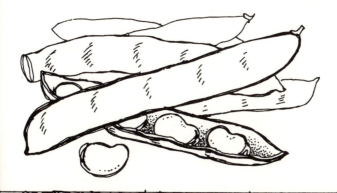

Mulligatawny Soup
(Serves 4-5)

For curry fans only. Follow with a light main course.

1 tablespoonful thin cooking oil
1 medium onion, peeled and sliced thinly
1 pint (550ml) water
10 raisins (approx.) or a few sultanas
1 medium carrot, scrubbed and sliced thinly
1 medium potato, peeled and cut into pieces
1 eating apple, peeled, cored and sliced
1 tablespoonful soy sauce
1 teaspoonful fresh lemon juice
1 oz (25g) natural flavour soy meat (mince) ground
in a coffee grinder
$\frac{1}{2}$ level teaspoonful mild curry powder
Sea salt

Fry the onion in the oil for two to three minutes. Add the water and all other ingredients except the salt. Bring to the boil and then simmer for seven to eight minutes. Allow to cool a little, then liquidize. Add salt to taste.

Filling. Gingery-brown in colour. Serve hot.

Fresh Pea Soup
(Serves 3-4)

Make this soup in June, July and August. In some areas a second crop of peas can be harvested in September. Frozen peas are not a patch on fresh ones, which you can be certain have not been dyed green or sweetened before they get to you.

1 medium onion
1 oz (25g) margarine
¾ lb (350g) peas after shelling
¾ pint (425ml) water
2 teaspoonsful soy sauce
Sea salt and freshly ground black pepper

Fry the onion in the margarine until transparent. Add half the water, the peas and the soy sauce. Bring to the boil and simmer with the lid on for about eight to ten minutes. Pour in the rest of the water and liquidize. Return to saucepan. Season to taste. Heat and serve.

Choose the best peas and the soup will be sweet-tasting and a beautiful green. Buy (or pick) 1½ lb (675g) pods to give you ¾ lb (350g) peas.

Fairly filling. Brilliant green in colour. Serve hot.

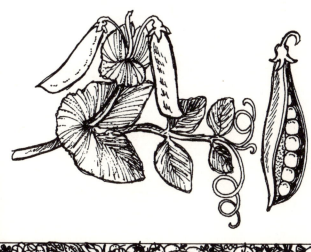

Peas and Carrots Soup

(Serves 4-5)

Make with new carrots and peas, in July. This soup simply bursts with flavour. As both peas and carrots are used, the result is a sweet tasting soup.

1 medium onion
1 heaped teaspoonful soft margarine
¾ lb (350g) peas in pod or about 6 oz (175g) shelled peas
½ lb (225g) small, new carrots, trimmed and sliced
3 teaspoonsful soy sauce
1 pint (550ml) water
Sea salt and freshly ground black pepper
1 heaped tablespoonful freshly chopped parsley

Fry the onion in the margarine for about three to four minutes. Add the peas, carrots, soy sauce and most of the water. Bring to the boil. Simmer for about ten to fifteen minutes and remove from heat. Add the rest of the water and liquidize. Return to saucepan. Taste and season. Sprinkle in the parsley. Heat and serve.

Fairly filling. Brownish-green in colour. Serve hot.

Sprout Soup
(Serves 4)

**1 medium-sized onion, peeled and sliced thinly
1 heaped teaspoonful soft margarine
1 medium potato, peeled and cut into thin pieces
10-12 sprouts, washed and prepared, cut into slices
1½ pints (850ml) water
1 tablespoonful soy sauce
Sea salt and freshly ground black pepper**

Fry the onion in the melted margarine for three to four minutes. Add the potato, sprouts, about 1 pint (550ml) of the water and the soy sauce. Bring to the boil and simmer with the lid on for 15 minutes. Add the rest of the water. Liquidize and return to saucepan. Taste and season. Reheat and serve immediately.

Not a soup that likes to be kept waiting. Good for times when sprouts are scarce.

Fairly filling. Very bright yellowy-green in colour. Serve hot.

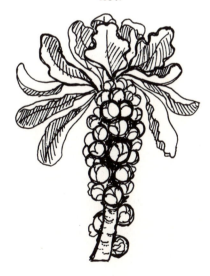

Celery and Cress Soup
(Serves 4)

A most unusual soup.

1 medium onion, peeled and sliced finely
1 tablespoonful thin cooking oil
4 stalks celery, washed, trimmed and cut into small
pieces
¾ pint (425ml) water
3 teaspoonsful soy sauce
1 carton cress – cut off just above the roots, washed in
a colander
1 level teaspoonful tomato *purée*
Sea salt and freshly ground black pepper

Fry the onion in the oil for three to four minutes. Put in the celery and gently stir-fry with the onion for about another three minutes. Pour the water into the liquidizer goblet. Add the celery and onion and blend. Return to the saucepan, bring to the boil and simmer for five minutes. Allow to cool a little, then strain through a fine mesh sieve. Pour back into the liquidizer goblet. Put in the prepared cress and blend. (Add a little more water if you think it is too thick.) Return to saucepan. Add the soy sauce and tomato *purée*. Stir in well, bring to the boil and simmer just for a minute while you taste and season. Serve immediately.

Fairly filling. Delicate green in colour. Serve hot.

Turnip Soup
(Serves 4)

Use only small new turnips.

1 large onion, peeled and sliced finely
1 tablespoonful thin cooking oil
1 lb (450g) small new turnips, trimmed, peeled and
sliced thinly
1½ pints (850ml) reconstituted dried milk (low fat)
1 tablespoonful soy sauce
Sea salt and freshly ground black pepper
4 slices wholewheat bread

Fry the onion in the oil for four to five minutes. Put in the turnip slices, milk and soy sauce. Bring to the boil (be very careful not to let it boil over) and simmer gently for about 25 minutes. Remove from heat and allow to cool a little. Liquidize and return to pan. Taste and season. Reheat gently, put a slice of wholewheat bread into each of four bowls. Pour the hot soup over these and serve.

Fairly filling. Creamy-white in colour. Serve hot.

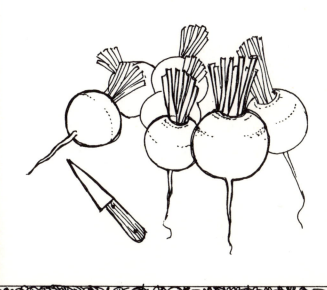

Cauliflower Soup
(Serves 2-3)

This is a rather subtle soup. Unless you really like cauliflower, this soup is not for you. Not a soup you can reheat or leave waiting. Make and serve immediately. Thick, creamy, palest green and unusual.

1 small onion, peeled and sliced finely
1 heaped teaspoonful soft margarine
¼ of the head of a medium cauliflower, washed (about 6 oz/175g)
green parts from 2 or 3 tender cauliflower leaves (discard stalks)
½ pint (275ml) water mixed with 1 heaped teaspoonful maize flour
Pinch freshly grated nutmeg
1 teaspoonful soy sauce
Sea salt and freshly ground black pepper

Use a large saucepan to fry the onion in the margarine. Cut the florets into small pieces with the greens and put into the saucepan. Pour in half the water. Bring to the boil and simmer for five minutes to soften. Remove from heat. Add the rest of the water. Liquidize and pour back into the saucepan. Add the soy sauce and nutmeg. Heat through and simmer for three minutes while stirring. Taste. Season. Serve hot, immediately.

Do not overdo the nutmeg. It should just round off the flavour. Choose a cauliflower with a really white head and springy greens, that smells good and fresh.

Fairly filling. Pale-creamy-green or greyish-cream in colour. Serve hot.

Avocado Soup
(Serves 2)

Serve immediately it is made, before it discolours. Avocado should be ripe, but not too soft.

1 small onion, peeled and sliced finely
2 teaspoonsful oil or 1 heaped teaspoonful margarine
1 medium-sized avocado pear, peeled, stone
removed, flesh chopped coarsely
2 teaspoonsful soy sauce
½ pint (275ml) water
Sea salt and freshly ground black pepper

Fry the onion gently in the oil or margarine. When it is transparent put into the blender with the avocado pieces, the soy sauce and water. Liquidize and return to saucepan. If it is too thick thin with water. Heat and simmer for three or four minutes. Season to taste and *serve immediately*, with wholewheat bread and margarine or butter.

This is a good way of using an avocado not quite ripe enough to serve as it is.

Fairly filling. Sage green in colour. Serve hot.

Carrot Soup
(Serves 2-3)

1 medium onion, peeled and sliced thinly
1 tablespoonful thin cooking oil
1 medium-sized stick of celery, trimmed, washed
and sliced
½ lb (225g) fresh carrots, trimmed, scrubbed and
sliced
¾ pint (425ml) water
2 teaspoonsful soy sauce
sugar, sea salt and freshly ground black pepper
1 heaped teaspoonful freshly chopped parsley

Fry the onion in the oil for two to three minutes. Put in the celery and carrot and fry lightly while stirring for a minute. (Use a wooden spoon.) Pour the water into the liquidizer goblet and spoon in the fried vegetables. Blend and return to the saucepan. Add the soy sauce, bring to the boil and then simmer for ten minutes with the lid on. Give it a stir occasionally. Taste. If it is slightly sweet (depending on the carrots), do not add any sugar. If it does not taste sweet then add a little Barbados sugar until it tastes right. Also add salt, pepper and the parsley.

Fairly light. Orange in colour. Serve hot.

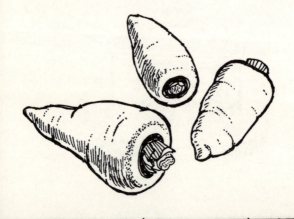

Beetroot Soup
(Serves 3)

Not a soup for beginners. The amount of vinegar added is crucial. Peeling the beetroot can be very messy as it stains the hands. However, the resulting soup, the colour of port, is worth it!

½ medium onion (or 1 small), peeled and sliced thinly
2 teaspoonsful thin cooking oil
1 stick celery, trimmed, scrubbed and chopped
about ½ lb (225g), after trimming, raw beetroot, cut into small pieces
¾ pint (425g) water
2 teaspoonsful soy sauce
1-2 teaspoonsful wine or cider vinegar
Sea salt and freshly ground black pepper
1 heaped tablespoonful cold cooked rice – optional
1 level teaspoonful maize flour
mixed with 2 tablespoonsful water

Fry the onion in the oil for three to four minutes. Add the celery, the beetroot pieces and about half the water. Bring to the boil and cook steadily with the lid on for 15 minutes for young beet or 20 minutes for older beet. Remove from heat. Add the rest of the water, soy sauce and liquidize. Strain through a fine metal sieve back into the saucepan. Add vinegar (start with ¼ teaspoonful) and salt and pepper to taste. When you are satisfied with the flavour, add the rice and the maize flour in water. Bring to the boil and simmer while stirring for three minutes.

Fairly light. Ruby-red in colour. Serve hot.

Bolognese Soup
(Serves 4)

**1 medium onion, peeled and sliced thinly
1 tablespoonful sunflower oil
1 clove garlic, peeled and crushed
(use a garlic crusher)
3 medium tomatoes, washed and sliced
2 medium mushrooms, washed and sliced
1 tablespoonful soy sauce
1 pint (550ml) water
1 level tablespoonful tomato *purée*
Sea salt and freshly ground black pepper
a little Barbados sugar (if needed)
grated cheese**

Fry the onion in the oil for three or four minutes. Add the crushed garlic, the tomatoes, mushrooms, soy sauce, the tomato *purée* and half the water. Bring to the boil and simmer gently with the lid on for ten minutes. Remove from heat. Add the rest of the water and liquidize. Return to heat. Taste and season with salt and pepper. Taste again. If it is too sour (depending on the tomatoes), add sugar by the pinch until it tastes right. Serve hot, sprinkled with grated cheese – Parmesan (if you can afford it).

To improve this soup, allow to stand for a few hours. Optional – add a little cooked pasta before reheating.

Fairly light. Browny-red in colour. Serve hot.

Cucumber and Spring Onion Soup
(Serves 4)

This does not taste a bit like one would imagine. A very unusual and interesting flavour. Make it when there is a glut of cucumbers.

6 small spring onions, trimmed and chopped
3 teaspoonsful thin cooking oil
½ large cucumber, peeled and chopped small
1 medium-sized potato, peeled and thinly sliced
1½ pints (850ml) water
3 teaspoonsful soy sauce
Sea salt and freshly ground black pepper

Put all the vegetables into a saucepan with 2 tablespoonsful of the water. Put the lid on and 'sweat' them for five minutes. Add the stock and most of the remaining water and bring to the boil. Simmer for about 20 minutes. Add the rest of the water. Liquidize and return to the saucepan. Taste and season. Reheat and serve.

Fairly light. Pale-green in colour. Serve hot.

Spinach Soup with Lemon
(Serves 4)

A very refreshing soup.

**1 shallot, peeled and finely chopped
3 teaspoonsful thin cooking oil
1 lb (450g) spinach, washed thoroughly, coarse stalks
torn away and discarded
1½ pints (850ml) water
3 teaspoonsful thin soy sauce
juice of ½ small lemon
Sea salt and freshly ground black pepper**

Fry the shallot in the oil for three to four minutes. Add about 1 pint (550ml) of the water, the spinach, cut into pieces and the soy sauce. Bring to the boil while you poke the spinach down with a wooden spoon. Simmer for 15-20 minutes with the lid off. Add the rest of the water and liquidize. Return to heat. Stir in the lemon juice. Taste and season.

Fairly light. Yellowy-green in colour. Serve hot.

Celery Soup
(Serves 4)

Thin. This soup definitely improves if left to stand for a few hours. Choose green celery and do not be afraid to use the tough outer stalks. Cut the celery into small pieces as the fibres tend to wrap round the blender blades.

1 medium onion, peeled and sliced
1 tablespoonful thin cooking oil
5-6 sticks celery, including the leaves,
washed and chopped small
½ pint (275ml) water
2 teaspoonsful soy sauce
Sea salt and freshly ground black pepper

Fry the onion in the oil for three to four minutes, gently so as not to brown it. Put in the celery and stir-fry with the onion for three minutes. Pour the water into the liquidizer goblet and spoon in the onion and celery. Blend. Return to saucepan, bring to the boil and simmer for five minutes. Allow to cool and blend. Strain back into the saucepan through a fine wire sieve. Press residue with the back of a wooden spoon. Add the soy sauce. Taste and season. Leave to stand a few hours. Reheat and serve with a sprinkle of grated cheese on top or with cheese straws.

Light. Pale yellowy-green in colour. Serve hot.

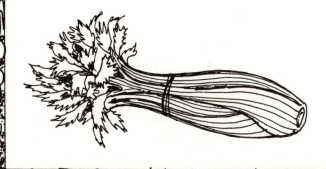

Green Soup
(Serves 2-3)

For the greens use cabbage (not white or red), sprout tops, spinach greens and sprouts. If you do not keep the lid on this soup while it is cooking you will put everybody off with its lingering smell. Prepare the greens – pick them over, cut away long stalks and discoloured leaves, wash thoroughly in plenty of cold water. Use a mixture of what is in season.

6 oz (175g) raw, prepared green, cut into pieces
½ oz (12g) margarine
½ medium onion, peeled and sliced thinly
½ pint (275ml) water
2 teaspoonsful soy sauce
Sea salt and freshly ground black pepper

Boil half of water in a saucepan and put in the prepared greens. Bring back to the boil and then simmer for six to eight minutes with the lid on to make them tender. In another saucepan fry the onion in the margarine, gently for three to four minutes. Put the water into the liquidizer goblet with the cooked onions, the cooked greens (and the water in which they were cooked). Blend and pour back into one of the saucepans. Add the soy sauce. Taste and season. Heat and serve *immediately*.

I admit this sounds a most peculiar soup, but if made with good, fresh greens it is really delicious. Serve immediately.

Light. Emerald-green in colour. Serve hot.

Clear Onion Soup

(Serves 4)

Depending on the onions this can be a very strong tasting soup. A good appetizer, so follow with a substantial main course.

**4 medium (or 2 large) onions,
peeled and sliced thinly
1 clove garlic, peeled and crushed
1½ tablespoonsful thin cooking oil
1½ pints (850ml) water
1 tablespoonful soy sauce
a little sugar to taste
Sea salt and freshly ground black pepper
2 heaped teaspoonsful finely chopped fresh parsley**

Fry the onion in the oil for about five minutes. Crush in the garlic. Add the water and the soy sauce and bring to the boil. Simmer gently, with the lid on, for about 20-25 minutes. Strain through a fine metal sieve, into a basin. (Discard the mushy onion slices.) Return the clear brown liquid to the saucepan. Add salt, pepper and sugar (by the pinch) to taste. Heat, sprinkle in the parsley and serve.

Very light. Transparent brown in colour. Serve hot.

Mushroom Soup
(Serves 4)

Small button mushrooms will give a subtle flavour and a pale pinkish colour. Larger mushrooms with dark brown gills will give a strong-bodied soup, dark brown and full of flavour. An all-the-year-round soup.

**1 medium onion, peeled and sliced
1 tablespoonful thin cooking oil
4 oz (100g) mushrooms, washed and sliced – do not peel
¾ pint (425ml) water
2 teaspoonsful soy sauce
Sea salt and freshly ground black pepper**

Fry the onion in the oil for three to four minutes. Put into the liquidizer with the mushrooms and soy sauce. Blend and pour into the saucepan. Bring to the boil and simmer for about five minutes. Taste and season. Serve on its own or with *croûtons*.

Light. Greyish-beige or greyish-brown in colour. Serve hot.

Leek Soup (thin)
(Serves 4)

Do not use just the white part of the leeks, use green as well.

1 medium onion, peeled and sliced thinly
1 tablespoonful thin cooking oil
1 lb (450g) leeks, trimmed of tough green and base,
sliced lengthways and washed thoroughly,
then cut into pieces
1½ pints (850ml) water
3 teaspoonsful soy sauce
Sea salt and freshly ground black pepper

Fry the onion in the oil for three to four minutes. Add the pieces of leek and stir for another three to four minutes. Pour in half the water and the 3 teaspoonsful soy sauce. Bring to the boil and simmer for about 15 minutes, with the lid on. Remove from heat, add a little of the remaining cold water and liquidize. (This is a very splashy soup, so be careful.) Return to saucepan and heat, using the last of the water if you need to thin it down. Taste and season.

Leeks are in season from November right through to April, so you can serve this soup for five months of the year. This is one of the most delicious soups I know.

Light. Delicate-green in colour. Serve hot.

TOMATO-BASE SOUPS

Here are three soups with a tomato base, ideal for when you have only a small amount of vegetables to use. Fresh tomato gives the most subtle results, but tinned Italian tomatoes are a good substitute, having a strong taste all their own. The tomato is really put in as part of the stock, to compliment the main vegetable and give a smooth texture. To avoid tomato pips, strain through a fine mesh sieve, after liquidizing. If you intend to strain the soup and you are using fresh tomatoes, do not bother to peel them. If the soup tastes a little sour, add a little Barbados sugar.

Leek and Tomato Soup
(Serves 4)

**1 medium onion, peeled and sliced thinly
1 tablespoonful thin cooking oil
2 medium-sized leeks, trimmed, split lengthways,
thoroughly washed and chopped into small pieces
4 medium-sized peeled and chopped fresh tomatoes,
or 4 tinned and a little juice
1 tablespoonful thin soy sauce
1 pint (550ml) water
Sea salt and freshly ground black pepper
Barbados sugar if needed**

Fry the leeks and the onion in the oil for four or five minutes, while stirring. Add the water and the soy sauce and bring to the boil. Simmer with the lid on for about 20 minutes. Remove from heat. Add the tomatoes. Pour into the liquidizer and blend for at least a minute. Put back into the saucepan. Bring to the boil again and simmer for three minutes. Taste and season. Serve hot.

Fairly filling. Browny-green in colour. Serve hot.

Mushroom and Tomato Soup

(Serves 4)

**1 medium onion, peeled and finely sliced
1 tablespoonful thin cooking oil
4 medium-sized mushrooms, washed and sliced
4 medium-sized fresh tomatoes,
peeled and chopped, or
4 tinned tomatoes plus a little juice
1 tablespoonful thin soy sauce
1 pint (550ml) water
Sea salt and freshly ground black pepper
Barbados sugar if needed**

Fry the onion in the oil for three to four minutes. Add the mushroom, the water and soy sauce. Bring to the boil and simmer for ten minutes. Add the tomatoes and liquidize. Pour back into the saucepan. Taste and season. Reheat and simmer for three minutes. Serve hot.

Fairly filling. Greyish-red in colour. Serve hot.

Spinach and Tomato Soup
(Serves 4)

To prepare spinach, rinse thoroughly in cold water. Tear the green away from the stalks (discard these) unless very young and tender leaves are used. Tear into small pieces.

1 medium onion, peeled and sliced thinly
1 tablespoonful thin cooking oil
½ lb (225g) prepared spinach
3 medium peeled tomatoes, chopped, or
three tinned tomatoes plus a little juice
3 teaspoonsful thin soy sauce
¾ pint (425ml) water
Sea salt and freshly ground black pepper

Fry the onion in the oil for three to four minutes. Stir in the spinach pieces, the water and the soy sauce. Bring to the boil and simmer for ten minutes. Remove from heat. Add the tomato and liquidize. Pour back into the saucepan. Bring to the boil again and simmer for three minutes. Taste and season. Serve hot.

This is not a soup for the beginner as it is not easy to get the seasoning just right. The spinach has a very metallic taste. If the flavour is too strong, thin down with water. If it gets completely out of hand, a few drops of lemon juice may help or a pinch or two of freshly grated nutmeg.

Fairly filling. Gingery-brown in colour. Serve hot.

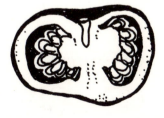

MIXED VEGETABLE SOUPS

'I can't be bothered' people say, 'It's so much easier to open a tin'. A sorry state of affairs! Fifty tins of vegetable soup all taste the same. Fifty home made vegetable soups will all be different. Tinned soup may be convenient, but it is also very dull and may not be very nourishing.

Here are twelve soup recipes made from a selection of mixed vegetables – one for each month of the year. Bear in mind that some vegetables are stored and are available all the year round. (Onions, carrots, potatoes.) Others have no particular season, thanks to imports and indoor growing methods – mushrooms, green peppers, cucumbers etc. The rest come fresh, when they are ready.

As the method for each of the soups is the same, to save repeating it twelve times, I will give you the basic instructions to start with.

Basic Method

Use a large saucepan to fry the onion in the oil. Add remaining vegetables and two-thirds of the water. Spoon in the soy sauce. Bring to the boil and simmer for about 15 minutes, with the lid on, until all the vegetables are tender. Remove from heat. Add the rest of the water and liquidize (in two lots if necessary). Return to pan. Heat through. Taste and season. Serve hot. (Dilute with more water if you find the soup too thick.)

Colours of the soups vary from greenish-brown to brown. Each of the soups will give enough for at least four servings.

January Vegetable Soup

What a month for vegetables this is – cabbage, sprouts, kale, cauliflower, celery, root vegetables, leeks … The temptation is to put too many vegetables in, but more than six will make it taste like 'everything soup'.

1 tablespoonful thin cooking oil
1 medium onion, peeled and sliced thinly
1 medium carrot, scrubbed and sliced
1 small parsnip, peeled and sliced
1 small turnip, peeled and sliced
4 sprouts, prepared and sliced
1 medium potato, peeled and sliced
1 pint (550ml) water
3 teaspoonsful soy sauce
Sea salt and freshly ground black pepper

See *Basic Method*. Optional: add two or three sprigs fresh parsley, washed and chopped finely, just before serving.

Filling. Serve hot.

February Vegetable Soup

1 tablespoonful thin cooking oil
1 medium onion, peeled and sliced thinly
1 medium carrot, scrubbed and sliced
1 medium leek, sliced through lengthways,
washed thoroughly and cut into pieces
1 stick celery
few sprigs cauliflower florets
1 pint (550ml) water – or more
1 tablespoonful soy sauce
Sea salt and freshly ground black pepper

See *Basic Method*.

Fairly filling. Serve hot.

March Vegetable Soup

1 tablespoonful thin cooking oil
2 medium onions, peeled and sliced thinly
¼ small swede, peeled and sliced
1 medium carrot, scrubbed and sliced
2 medium mushrooms, washed and sliced
4 sprouts, prepared and sliced or a slice from fresh
green cabbage, washed and chopped
1 pint (550ml) water – or more
1 tablespoonful soy sauce
1 heaped teaspoonful tomato *purée*
Sea salt and freshly ground black pepper

See *Basic Method*. Add the *purée* with the soy sauce.

Fairly filling. Serve hot.

April Vegetable Soup

1 tablespoonful thin cooking oil
1 medium onion, peeled and sliced
6 spinach leaves, (with stalk cut out)
washed well and torn into pieces
few cauliflower florets
1 medium carrot, scrubbed and sliced
2 small leeks, sliced through, washed
thoroughly and cut into pieces
1 pint (550ml) water – or more
3 teaspoonsful soy sauce
Sea salt and freshly ground black pepper

See *Basic Method*. Serve with sippets.

Fairly filling. Serve hot.

May Vegetable Soup

This month is usually the leanest for soup vegetables, so it is time to use salad vegetables.

1 tablespoonful thin cooking oil
1 medium onion, peeled and finely sliced
1 small carrot, scrubbed and sliced
2 medium mushrooms, washed and sliced
¼ cucumber, washed and sliced
2 medium tomatoes, sliced
1 pint (550ml) water – or more
3 teaspoonsful soy sauce
1 heaped teaspoonful tomato *purée*
4 sprigs parsley, washed and chopped finely

See *Basic Method*.

Light. Serve hot.

June Vegetable Soup

This month usually brings several new items to the greengrocers. Keep back a few peas and broad beans from the vegetables you buy for your main course.

1 tablespoonful thin cooking oil
2 small onions, peeled and thinly sliced
3 small new potatoes, washed and sliced
broad beans from 2 or 3 pods
peas from 6-8 pods
2 outside lettuce leaves,
washed and cut into pieces
3 medium tomatoes
1 pint (550ml) water – or more
1 tablespoonful soy sauce
2-3 pinches sugar
Sea salt and freshly ground black pepper

See *Basic Method*. Add the sugar with the seasoning. (If the tomatoes are sweet, you may not need it.)

Fairly filling. Serve hot.

July Vegetable Soup

1 tablespoonful thin cooking oil
1 medium onion, peeled and sliced thinly
1 courgette, stalk cut off, washed and sliced
2-3 baby carrots, topped and tailed,
washed and sliced
1 tablespoonful raw peas
2 small new potatoes, scrubbed and sliced
2 small button mushrooms, washed and sliced
1 pint (550ml) water
1 tablespoonful soy sauce
Sea salt and freshly ground black pepper

See *Basic Method*.

Fairly filling. Serve hot.

August Vegetable Soup

1 tablespoonful thin cooking oil
1 medium onion, peeled and sliced thinly
4 runner beans, washed, topped and tailed and
strings removed, cut into small pieces
1 medium carrot, scrubbed and sliced
1 small turnip, peeled and sliced
4 small tomatoes
4 cauliflower florets washed
1 pint (550ml) water
1 tablespoonful soy sauce
Sea salt and freshly ground black pepper

See *Basic Method*. If you prefer, use french beans, instead of runners – just top and tail, strings can stay on. Cauliflower can be left out if preferred.

Filling. Serve hot.

September Vegetable Soup

1 tablespoonful thin cooking oil
1 medium onion, peeled and sliced thinly
2 sticks celery, trimmed, washed and chopped
2 tomatoes, washed and sliced
1 medium carrot, scrubbed and sliced
2 runner beans, washed, topped and tailed,
strings removed, cut into small pieces
$\frac{1}{2}$ small cucumber, washed and chopped
few shelled broad beans, if any
1 pint (550ml) water
1 tablespoonful thin soy sauce
Sea salt and ground black pepper

See *Basic Method*.

Fairly filling. Serve hot.

October Vegetable Soup

1 tablespoonful thin vegetable oil
1 medium onion, peeled and sliced thinly
1 medium potato, peeled and sliced
1 medium carrot, scrubbed and sliced
1 cabbage leaf, washed and cut into small pieces
1 tablespoonful soy sauce
2 heaped teaspoonsful tomato *purée*
1 pint (550ml) water – or more
2-3 sprigs parsley, washed and finely chopped
Sea salt and freshly ground black pepper

See *Basic Method*. Put in the *purée* the same time as the soy sauce. Sprinkle in the parsley just before serving. The potato makes this a thick creamy soup.

Fairly filling. Serve hot.

November Vegetable Soup

**1 tablespoonful thin cooking oil
1 medium onion, peeled and sliced thinly
1 stick celery, scrubbed and chopped
1 small parsnip, peeled and sliced
1 small turnip, peeled and sliced
4 sprouts, prepared and sliced
1-2 medium-sized mushrooms, washed and sliced
1 pint (550ml) water – or more
1 tablespoonful soy sauce
Sea salt and freshly ground black pepper**

See *Basic Method*.

Fairly filling. Serve hot.

December Vegetable Soup

1 tablespoonful thin cooking oil
1 medium onion, peeled and sliced
1 medium carrot, trimmed, scrubbed and sliced
small chunk of peeled swede, sliced
green from 3-4 spinach leaves, washed well
and cut into pieces
few broccoli florets, or 2-3 sprouts, prepared and
sliced
1 small clove garlic, peeled and crushed
1 tablespoonful soy sauce
1 pint (550ml) water – or more
Sea salt and freshly ground black pepper

See *Basic Method*. Add the garlic with the soy sauce.

Fairly filling. Serve hot.

Making Up Your Own Hot Vegetable Soup Recipes

Here are some points to bear in mind.

1. Start all soups with onion fried in oil or margarine.
2. Do not put more than six different vegetables in the soup.
3. Suggested stock/flavourings:
   soy sauce
   tomato *purée* or tinned tomatoes
   garlic (fresh)
   sea salt
   freshly ground black pepper
4. Soup that has turned out too sweet can be unsweetened with a few drops lemon juice (fresh).
5. Potato will make soup both thick and creamy.
6. To thicken a soup that is too thin, put up to 1 *level* tablespoonful maize flour into a cup with 2 tablespoonsful cold water. Mix to a smooth paste and add to hot soup. Bring to the boil and simmer while stirring for two or three minutes. Maize flour has a bland taste and so does not affect the flavour.
7. Soup which is too thick can be diluted with water. Adjust stock and seasoning after diluting.
8. Always taste *before* seasoning.
9. If your soup goes completely wrong and tastes horrible, throw it away. Don't be unkind and make other people eat it – think of your reputation!
10. Serve hot soup in warmed bowls or soup plates.
11. Remember the old saying, 'A soup boiled is a soup spoiled' – how very true! Merely *bring to the boil*, then simmer.

Mixed Vegetable Broth (thin)

Take any one of the ingredient lists for vegetable soups, according to season.

The method is the same for all kinds of vegetable broth. Chop the onion finely and fry in the oil. Dice all the other vegetables (except peas) and put into the saucepan with all the water, soy sauce and tomato *purée* if used. Bring to the boil and simmer for 20-25 minutes. By this time the vegetables will be soft right through and even mushy. Strain through a fine wire sieve, using a wooden spoon and a bowl. Aim to just squeeze the juice from the vegetables. Discard the residue in the sieve. Put the liquid you have collected (in the bowl) in the saucepan. Heat through. Season and add a sprinkle of freshly chopped parsley. Serve hot with either cooked rice (a heaped tablespoonful) or a sprinkle of chopped noodles, sippets, or pancake strips. (See section on soup accompaniments, p.26).

The rather dull colour and texture of this broth is improved by the inclusion of the rice etc. The flavour is excellent. An ideal soup to start a meal that has a substantial main course.

A very light soup. Transparent brown in colour. Serve hot.

Hot Nut Soups

Almond Soup
(Serves 3)

As the almonds contain oil, the onion is not fried in extra oil as it would make the soup too greasy. Use shelled almonds and not bought ground almonds.

2 oz (50g) shelled almonds, brown skins left on
1 small onion, peeled and finely chopped
1 large stalk celery, washed and chopped small
1 pint (550ml) water
3 teaspoonsful soy sauce
1 level teaspoonful maize flour
1 heaped teaspoonful dried milk granules,
dissolved in ¼ pint (150ml) cold water
Sea salt and freshly ground black pepper

Grind the almonds in an electric grinder. Put into a saucepan with the finely chopped onion and celery. Mix the maize flour with a little of the water. When all the lumps have gone add the rest of the water and the soy sauce. Pour into the pan with the almonds, onion and celery. Bring to the boil and simmer with the lid on for about 25-30 minutes. Strain into a bowl, through a fine mesh sieve. Heat the thick milk and add to the soup. Taste and season.

Fairly filling. Dull-beige, sometimes pink-beige in colour. Serve hot.

Walnut Soup
(Serves 4)

**4 oz (100g) walnuts, shelled and freshly ground,
as fine as possible
1 small clove garlic, peeled and
put through a garlic press
¼ pint (150ml) reconstituted dried milk plus
1 heaped tablespoonful extra dried milk,
mixed in well (no lumps)
3 teaspoonsful soy sauce
1½ pints (850ml) water
Sea salt and freshly ground black pepper**

Put the nuts into a mortar with the garlic and a tablespoonful of the milk and pound to a smooth paste. Put into a saucepan with the rest of the thick milk, soy sauce and water. Heat gently while stirring. Taste and season. Serve hot.

Filling. Unpredictable greyish-brown colour. Serve hot.

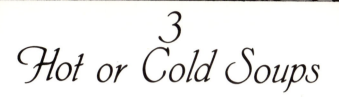

3
Hot or Cold Soups

Apricot and Cucumber Soup
(Serves 2-3)

3 oz (75g) dried apricots
juice from ½ lemon
¾ pint (425ml) water
2 teaspoonsful Barbados sugar
½ cucumber, peeled and chopped finely
1 small onion, peeled and chopped finely
1 tablespoonful thin cooking oil
½ teaspoonful mild curry powder
Sea salt

Grate the rind from the lemon into a saucepan. Add the cold water and apricots. Leave to soak overnight. Bring to the boil, add the sugar and simmer for 15-20 minutes. Allow to cool. Liquidize to a smooth *purée*. Put the cucumber and onion into a pan and pour in the oil. Fry gently for about five minutes. Add the apricot *purée* and the curry powder. Bring to the boil and simmer gently for ten minutes. Taste and add salt. Thin with more water if required.

Fairly filling. Brownish colour. Served hot or chilled.

Watercress Soup (thin)
(Serves 3)

A rich dark green soup, full of flavour.

1 medium onion, peeled and sliced finely
1 oz (25g) margarine
1 bunch watercress (including stems),
washed thoroughly and coarsely chopped
(discard any discoloured parts)
¾ pint (425ml) water
2 teaspoonsful soy sauce
Sea salt

Fry the onion in the margarine until transparent. (Don't let it brown.) Put the onion, watercress and about half the water into the liquidizer. Blend. Return to the saucepan. Add the rest of the water and the soy sauce. Bring to the boil and simmer for ten minutes.

Light. Deep-green in colour. Serve hot or cold.

Fresh Tomato Soup
(Serves 4 generously)

Can be served hot or chilled as it is slightly sweet. A very splashy soup – be careful when liquidizing.

1 medium onion
1 oz (25g) margarine
1 lb (450g) tomatoes, skinned and chopped
1 pint (550ml) water
2 teaspoonsful soy sauce
Barbados sugar to taste
Sea salt and freshly ground black pepper
2 heaped teaspoonsful chopped parsley

Stab the tomatoes with a fork and hold each one in a basin of boiling water for a few seconds while the skin splits and loosens. Cool in cold water and peel. Fry the onion in the margarine for three to four minutes. Add the tomatoes and about half the water. Pour into the liquidizer goblet with the soy sauce and blend. Return to the saucepan and add the rest of the water. Heat through and simmer for two to three minutes. Taste. If sour, then add sugar, a pinch at a time until it tastes right. (If tomatoes are sweet there is no need to add any sugar.) Season with salt and pepper. Serve hot sprinkled with the parsley. Can also be served chilled, slightly sweeter.

Light. Pale apricot/orange in colour. Serve hot or cold.

Green Pepper and Tomato Soup
(Serves 4)

1 medium onion, peeled and sliced thinly
1 tablespoonful sunflower oil
1 clove garlic, peeled and crushed
2 medium-sized green peppers,
washed de-seeded and with the stalk removed,
chopped into smallish pieces
4 medium tomatoes, sliced
1 teaspoonful Barbados sugar
1 tablespoonful soy sauce
1 pint (550ml) water
2 heaped teaspoonsful freshly chopped parsley
Sea salt and freshly ground black pepper

Fry the onion in the oil for two or three minutes. Add the crushed garlic and stir well. Put in the chopped peppers, sliced tomatoes, sugar, soy sauce and about half the water. Bring to the boil and simmer for five minutes. Add the remainder of the water and liquidize. (You may have to do this in two lots.) Return to saucepan through a fine wire sieve. (Discard residue.) Add the chopped parsley. Stir well and season to taste.

Some people might find this soup a little thin, although it is opaque. If you want to thicken it add 1 level tablespoonful maize flour and 2 tablespoonsful cold water, mixed well. Put this in at the final heating. Bring to the boil and simmer for three minutes while stirring. This is a soup that can actually improve if allowed to stand for a few hours so don't be afraid to make it well in advance and heat or chill when you want to serve it.

Light. Ginger in colour. Serve hot or cold.

Courgette Soup
(Serves 4)

Full of surprises – it looks like a really thick soup, but is extremely light and refreshing with a slightly sweet taste. In season for only a few weeks of the year. As nice cold as it is hot and a most appropriate start to a summer meal. Follow with a substantial main course and a light fresh fruit sweet such as raspberries.

**1 medium onion, peeled and finely chopped
1 heaped teaspoonful soft margarine
1 lb (450g) baby marrows, washed and with the
stalks cut off
3 teaspoonsful thin soy sauce
½ pint (275ml) cold water
seasoning**

Fry the onion in the margarine, in a medium-sized saucepan. When transparent add the marrows, sliced, the soy sauce and about half the water. Bring to the boil and simmer for seven to eight minutes with the lid off. (Give a stir once or twice while cooking.) Remove from heat and add the rest of the water. Liquidize and return to saucepan. Taste. Season with sea salt and freshly ground black pepper.

Light. Palest-green with flecks of dark green. Serve hot or cold from the fridge.

4
Cold Soups

A few of the soups in this book can be eaten hot or cold, but in general cold soups require an entirely different approach. Serve all cold soups chilled from the fridge. Most of them need some kind of thickened base which you can then flavour with fruit or vegetable, *purée*, yogurt, milk or sometimes a liquid thickened with maize flour or potato will do.

Cool Green Soup
(Serves 3-4)

This is especially nice for hot June, July and August days, when spinach and lettuce are at their best.

1 small onion, peeled and sliced thinly
2 teaspoonsful thin cooking oil
3 small new potatoes, washed thoroughly and sliced
thinly
1 pint (550ml) water
2 teaspoonsful thin soy sauce
handful spinach leaves, washed thoroughly and
whole stalks removed
about 12 fresh mint leaves, washed
Sea salt and freshly ground black pepper

Fry the onion in the oil for three or four minutes. Add the thin potato slices, about three-quarters of the water, the soy sauce and all the leaves. Bring to the boil while you poke the leaves down with a wooden spoon. Simmer with the lid off for about 15 minutes. Add the rest of the water and liquidize. Pour back into the saucepan through a fine mesh metal sieve. Taste and season. Allow to cool and then chill in the fridge (in a jug) for about four hours before serving.

Fairly light, colour bright green. Serve cold.

Gazpacho
(Serves 4-5)

This is a cold soup which originated in Spain. Make it when there is a glut of tomatoes. A nice soup for a sweltering summer evening.

**4 large tomatoes, washed, skinned and coarsley
chopped
6 spring onions, trimmed and sliced
1 clove garlic, peeled and crushed
½ medium cucumber, peeled and chopped
cold water
2 teaspoonsful thin cooking oil
Sea salt and freshly ground black pepper**

Accompaniments
**1 small green or red pepper,
washed, stem and seeds removed, diced
¼ cucumber, washed and diced
2 slices fresh wholewheat bread, cut into cubes
1 small onion, peeled and finely chopped**

Put the tomatoes, spring onions, crushed garlic and cucumber into the liquidizer. Add a little water and blend to a smooth pulp. Put in the oil and as much water as you think will make a medium-thick consistency. Blend again. Taste and season. Put into the fridge for an hour or two to chill thoroughly. Also chill the soup dishes. Serve from the fridge with the accompaniments. These should be handed round in bowls (with spoons) for people to sprinkle into their bowls of cold soup.

If you make this too thin it can be thickened by adding half a slice of wholewheat bread (crusts removed), and blending again in the liquidizer. Put in all the soup and the bread broken into small pieces.

Fairly filling. Pale-brown in colour. Serve cold.

Vichyssoise
(Serves 4)

A cold, creamy, leek soup.

This soup is most abused by restaurant chefs who open a tin of leek soup and mix it with cream. The result is disgustingly rich and not a bit like the real thing. Small, young leeks are best.

**1 small onion, peeled and sliced
1 heaped teaspoonful soft margarine
1 lb (450g) leeks – trim and use only the white parts,
washed thoroughly, sliced finely
2 medium-sized potatoes, peeled and sliced thinly
1 pint (550ml) water
3 teaspoonsful thin soy sauce
Sea salt and freshly ground black pepper
4 tablespoonsful thin cream
1 heaped tablespoonful washed and chopped chives**

Melt the margarine in a saucepan and put in the onion and leeks. Fry gently for about five minutes while stirring. Add the potato slices and about 1 pint (550ml) of the water. Put the lid on and simmer gently for about 30 minutes. Liquidize. Stir in the soy sauce. Taste and season. If you think it is too thick, stir in a little more water. Allow to grow cold. Stir in the cream. Chill in the fridge for about one hour. Serve cold, sprinkled with chives.

Cream can be omitted if amount of potato is increased. Use an extra potato and a little bit more water.

Filling. Pale cream in colour. Serve cold.

Lettuce Soup
(Serves 4)

2 medium-sized onions, peeled and sliced thinly
1 tablespoonful thin cooking oil
1 average size lettuce including all good outside
leaves
(remove small heart leaves and use for something
else), washed thoroughly in cold water
2 medium-sized potatoes, peeled and sliced thinly
1½ pints (850ml) water
1 tablespoonful soy sauce
Sea salt and freshly ground black pepper

Fry the onions in the oil. Add the lettuce cut into small
pieces. Fry very gently so that it does not brown. Add the
potato slices, about 1 pint (550ml) of the water and the
tablespoonful of soy sauce. Bring to the boil and simmer
for about ten minutes with the lid on. Add the rest of the
water and liquidize. Pour back into the saucepan, season
and serve hot with sippets.

Fairly filling. Palest-green in colour. Serve cold.

Cucumber Soup

$\frac{1}{2}$ medium-sized cucumber, peeled and chopped
small carton of natural yogurt or (better still)
equivalent of home-made yogurt
chilled milk
2-3 mint leaves, chopped very finely
Sea salt and freshly ground black pepper

Put the yogurt and the cucumber into the liquidizer and blend. Thin down with chilled milk. Stir in the chopped mint and season to taste. Serve cold from the fridge with a thin slice of cucumber floating in the middle.

Fairly filling. Palest-green in colour. Serve cold.

Parsley Soup

(Serves 3)

**1 small onion peeled and sliced thinly
1 heaped teaspoonful vegetable margarine
2 oz (50g) parsley, washed (stems discarded) finely
chopped
2 medium potatoes, peeled and sliced thinly
3 teaspoonsful soy sauce
1 pint (550ml) skimmed milk
Sea salt and freshly ground black pepper**

Fry the onion in the margarine for three to four minutes, with the lid on. Add the potato and parsley. Stir for a minute or two and then add the milk and soy sauce. Bring to the boil and simmer with the lid on for half an hour. Remove from heat and allow to cool for a few minutes. Blend and return to saucepan. Taste, season and add a little water if you think it is too thick. Allow to cool and then put into the fridge, in a jug, to chill. Pour out and serve.

Fairly filling. Pale-green in colour. Serve cold.

Carrot and Orange Soup
(Serves 3)

1 medium onion, peeled and sliced finely
1 tablespoonful thin cooking oil
1 heaped teaspoonful 100 per cent wholewheat flour
¾ pint (425ml) water
2 teaspoonsful thin soy sauce
½ pint (275ml) orange juice
1 tablespoonful washed, finely chopped chives
Sea salt and freshly ground black pepper
2 good pinches grated nutmeg
2 good pinches ground allspice
½ lb (225g) carrots, washed and chopped

Fry the onion gently in the oil for three to four minutes.
Sprinkle in the flour and cook while stirring for a minute.
Remove from heat and stir in the water, soy sauce and
orange juice. Bring to the boil and simmer for about
three minutes until thickened. Add the chives, two to
three pinches salt, a sprinkle of pepper, the nutmeg and
allspice. Stir well. Add the chopped carrots, bring to the
boil again and simmer with the lid on for 20-25 minutes,
until carrots are tender. Remove from heat and liquidize
when cool enough. Allow to get cold and then chill in the
fridge.

Fairly light. Orange in colour. Serve cold.

Cold Fruit Soups

Cold fruit soups originated in Scandinavia. Basically they are (stewed) fruit *purées*, slightly sweetened and spiced with cinnamon, nutmeg and allspice. If the fruit *purée* is too thin, cornflour can be used for thickening. The soups should not be too sweet, but slightly tart and served chilled from the fridge.

Choose from apples, blackberries, apricots, raspberries, loganberries, plums, greengages, black-currants, redcurrants, damsons, gooseberries etc. (single fruits or combinations). Prepare fruit and stew in water, enough to cover fruit. Bring to the boil and simmer until soft. Allow to cool. Remove stones. Liquidize and sweeten (not too much) to taste. If the *purée* is thin, use up to 1 level tablespoonful of maize flour to 1 pint (550ml) *purée*. Blend the cornflour with a little of the *purée*. Pour back into the rest of the *purée* and bring to the boil. Simmer for three to four minutes until *purée* has thickened. Allow to cool. Add a pinch or two of one or all the spices if you think it necessary. Mix in well. Serve chilled from the fridge in squat tumblers, on a saucer with a spoon.

If you would like to use cherries, stone them first with a cherry stoner. For fruit such as plums with thick skins, put the *purée*, after liquidizing, through a fine mesh metal sieve. This also applies to fruits with tiny pips such as raspberries and loganberries. Discard residue.

If you only have a small amount of fruit, extend the soup with orange juice (fresh).

One of the main attractions of this type of soup is the brilliant colour it can add to a meal.

Starters

Starters

As lovely as soups are, sometimes it is nice to start with either a drink from a glass or something more solid. Starters feature more fruits than soups and also more of the proteins valuable to vegetarians – eggs, nuts and cheese.

The message is the same for this section – good fresh food, wholesome and nutritious!

5
Cold Starters

Crudités

This rather ugly word describes one of the easiest and yet best kinds of starter to any meal. *The vegetables must be of the very best quality and really fresh*. The nicest way to serve is one plate per person with a small dish in the centre. Fill this with a dressing of some kind, such as the ones following this recipe. Around the dressing arrange the following washed 'nibbles':

> small florets of raw cauliflower
> twigs of raw carrot
> twigs of celery
> whole radishes
> prepared spring onions
> small, whole tomatoes
> small heart leaves of cos lettuce
> sprigs of washed watercress

These are eaten (using the fingers) dipped in dressing. Allow about three teaspoonsful of dressing per person and two of at least four items from the list.

Fairly filling.

Salad Dressing

2 heaped teaspoonsful made mustard
2 tablespoonsful cider or wine vinegar
4 tablespoonsful sunflower oil
4 grinds of black pepper
large pinch sea salt
2 teaspoonsful Barbados sugar

Put all ingredients into a screw top jar. Make sure the lid is on and shake vigorously. Shake before serving.

Lemon Salad Dressing

1 tablespoonful fresh lemon juice
3 tablespoonsful sunflower oil
1 teaspoonful Barbados sugar
pinch sea salt
1 grind black pepper

Put all the ingredients into a screw top jar. Make sure the lid is on firmly and shake vigorously to blend. Shake again before serving.

Citrus Salad

For each person you will need:

$\frac{1}{2}$ **grapefruit**
$\frac{1}{2}$ **large orange**
Barbados sugar

Wash and dry the fruit (whole). Cut off a flat slice top and bottom, right through to the flesh. Peel, making sure you remove both pith and rind. Do not waste the juice while you are doing this. (Hold the fruit over a bowl.) Using a sharp knife, cut between the dividing membranes so that you get wedges of juicy flesh. Let the wedges fall into the bowl. Squeeze out any remaining juice from the waste membrane. Arrange alternate slices of grapefruit and orange on a flat plate. Sprinkle with a little brown sugar. Serve with a spoon and fork.

Very light.

Avocado and Grapefruit Salad

For each person you will need one third to a half avocado and one third to a half grapefruit, depending on size of fruit. Prepare the grapefruit first as for citrus salad. Peel the avocado, cut in half lengthways and pull apart to remove large stone. Slice and arrange alternately with grapefruit on a flat plate.

This is not to everyone's taste, being rather sharp. The juice from the grapefruit should stop the avocado slices from turning brown.

Avocado Vinaigrette

For each person allow half an average-sized avocado. Wash and dry the fruit. Slice in half lengthways. Pull apart carefully and remove the stone. Put into dishes, cut side upwards, spoon vinaigrette over and into the hole left by the stone. If you do not have the specially shaped avocado dishes, cut off a little slice underneath for them to balance on. Serve with a teaspoon and small slivers of thin brown bread and margarine or butter. (Ask someone knowledgeable to show you how to pick an exactly ripe avocado if you cannot do it yourself – if you press the skin lightly, the flesh inside it should feel slightly soft.)

Mayonnaise

This is less rich than the usual kind of mayonnaise. Avocado pears are very high in saturated fat, so the usual kind is a little too heavy.

1 level teaspoonful soya flour
1 tablespoonful wine vinegar
4 tablespoonsful sunflower oil
Sea salt and freshly ground black pepper to taste
1 teaspoonful Barbados sugar

Put the soya flour into a basin with the vinegar and mix to a smooth paste with a teaspoon. Then put all ingredients into a screw top jar. Fasten lid firmly and shake well.

Optional extra: 2 heaped teaspoonsful very finely chopped mild onion.

Almond Pâté with Toast

(Serves 4)

4 oz (100g) ground almonds (fresh)
2 tablespoonsful sunflower oil
2 teaspoonsful (slightly heaped) tomato *purée*
½ teaspoonful or more of fresh lemon juice
Sea salt and freshly ground black pepper

Use a small basin to blend the almonds and oil. Add the tomato *purée* and lemon juice. Mix to a smooth paste. Season to taste. Serve spread thickly on freshly toasted wholemeal bread. Garnish with fresh parsley sprigs.

This is only a very simple recipe, but is really delicious.

Very filling (because of oil content).

Walnut Pâté with Toast

(Serves 4)

2 oz (50g) soft margarine
1 oz (25g) finely chopped onion
2 oz (50g) split pea flour
6 fl.oz. (175ml) water
5 oz (150g) ground walnuts
1 level teaspoonful finely chopped thyme
2 heaped teaspoonsful tomato *purée*
2 teaspoonsful lemon juice
Sea salt and freshly ground black pepper

Gently melt the margarine in a saucepan. Add the onion and fry for three to four minutes, stirring. Tip in the pea flour and mix until all the margarine has been absorbed. Fry this for about two minutes, stirring with a wooden spoon. Remove from heat. Pour on the water. Put back over heat and cook for another three to four minutes, breaking up any lumps, until you have a stiff paste. Add the walnuts, lemon juice, *purée* and herb. Mix well and season to taste. Serve hot, piled into the centres of warm plates with triangles of hot wholemeal toast. Serve margarine or butter separately. (Fresh or dried thyme will do.)

Very filling.

Mushrooms à la Grecque
(Serves 4)

**1 oz (25g) grated onion
2 tablespoonsful sunflower oil
glass dry white wine
1 small clove garlic, peeled
Sea salt and freshly ground black pepper
12 oz (350g) button mushrooms
4 medium-sized tomatoes
freshly chopped parsley**

Fry the onion in the oil. Add the wine and crushed garlic (use a garlic press). Wash the mushrooms and leave whole. Stab each tomato with a fork and plunge them in boiling water until they split and you can peel them easily. Put the mushrooms and quartered, peeled tomatoes into the onion mixture. Cook for about ten minutes until half the liquid remains. Season to taste. Leave to cool. Chill and serve in small dishes plus a sprinkle of parsley.

Note. If you do not want to use wine, try apple juice instead (the non-fizzy kind).

Fairly filling. Serve cold.

Melon (Charantais or Ogen)

If small, serve one melon per person. Wash and dry. Cut through the fruit horizontally about half way down. Remove this lid and scoop out the seeds with a spoon from both pieces. Serve on a plate with a spoon and fork. Larger fruit can be cut in half, horizontally through the middle and half a melon served per person.

Fairly light depending on size of melon. Serve cold.

Melon (green or yellow hard skin types)

Wash and dry. Cut out wedges with a sharp knife. Slice into cubes as shown. Either leave them on the skin or put just the cubes into a glass dish. Some people prefer a little powdered ginger sprinkled over the cubes just before serving. Serve chilled. Alternatively, cut into thin wedges removing skin. Lay on a plate in a fan shape. Serve with a small knife and fork.

Fairly light. Serve cold.

Bean and Onion Salad

For each person you will need:

**4 oz (100g) cold, cooked green beans –
runners, french or string (see section on hot
vegetables for cooking instructions, p.00)
2-3 teaspoonsful vinaigrette
Sea salt and freshly ground black pepper
1 heaped teaspoonful finely chopped spring onion**

Put the cold beans in a shallow dish. Add vinaigrette and
seasoning. Sprinkle with the onion.

Fairly light. Serve cold.

Pea and Onion Salad

As bean and onion salad except use 4 oz (100g) cooked
peas instead of beans.

Fairly filling. Serve cold.

Radishes and Wholewheat Bread

For each person allow seven to nine radishes. Trim off stalk and long root. Wash. Cut as shown and put into iced water for a few minutes to open out. Dry and serve with thin slices of wholewheat bread and margarine or butter.

Light (if not too much bread is served). Serve cold.

Tomatoes and Wholewheat Bread

If you are lucky enough to grow your own tomatoes, or someone makes you a present of home-grown ones, do not waste them in a salad! Wash and quarter, serving two medium tomatoes per person. Serve with wholewheat bread and margarine or butter. Firm, sweet, exceptionally good fruit is best for this starter.

Light (if not too much bread is served). Serve cold.

Fresh Fruit Juices

These should be served cold or chilled from the fridge. I suppose orange is the most useful fresh fruit juice. It is universally popular and makes a very good base for a mixed-flavour fruit juice. Allow two medium-sized oranges per person and extract their juice, on a citrus juicer a few minutes before you serve, for the best results and the most compliments. You should not need to add sweetening. Tangerine and satsuma can be treated in the same way.

Grapefruit is another popular citrus fruit. Allow one

small grapefruit per person. Sweeten with a little Barbados sugar or runny honey to taste.

The following can be *puréed* in the blender with a little water and their juice strained: strawberries (first washed and hulled), raspberries (washed), fresh pineapple (cut into slices, the outside trimmed off and the core cut out), melon (flesh only cut into cubes), seedless grapes (washed), dessert pear (washed, peeled, sliced), apple (washed, peeled, sliced), cherries (washed, stoned), ripe apricot (washed, stoned), peach (washed, peeled, stoned).

Stewing fruit such as apricot, greengage, plum, gooseberry, blackberry, redcurrant, blackcurrant etc. can be used for fruit juice. Stew the fruit in the usual way with sugar and water. When soft, press as much through a fine mesh wire sieve as you can. The resulting juice can be diluted with a little water if too thick.

Dried fruit can also be used for juice. Soak overnight in water so that it swells up. Use apricots, peaches, prunes, pears, sultanas, raisins. Liquidize in a little more water and strain off the juice. (Remember to cut out any stones before liquidizing.) Bear in mind that dried fruit has lost all its vitamin C.

If very thin, serve your fruit juice in a glass with an ice cube. For slightly thicker ones, serve in a glass, on a saucer with a teaspoon.

Make up your fruit juices first, taste them and sweeten if necessary. Do not make them too sweet if using as a starter. Dilute, if you think a juice is too thick, using water or thin juice.

Here is a list of fruit cocktails you can make quite easily.

1. 2 parts from orange juice to 1 part juice of any one of the following:

apricots (stewed)
greengages
blackberries
redcurrants
blackcurrants
Sweeten to taste. Serve cold.

2. 3 parts fresh orange to 1 part blended and strained juice of any one of the following:
strawberries
pineapple
raspberries
cherries
pear
Sweeten to taste. Serve cold.

3. 2 parts fresh orange or grapefruit to 1 part blended and strained juice of:
prunes
apricots
sultanas
raisins
Add a few drops of lemon juice too. Sweeten to taste and serve cold.

If you want to be more adventurous make up your own combinations bearing these points in mind.

—— Blend not more than three juices.
—— Use strong flavours for the least amount required.
—— Make one juice a base for your cocktail – orange, grapefruit, pineapple or grape are ideal.
—— Make just before you serve. Do not keep fruit juices hanging around in the fridge.
—— Keep a note of successful fruit cocktails so you can make them again.

6
Hot Starters

Hot Grapefruit

For each person allow half a grapefruit. Choose fruit which feel heavy for their size – these have the most juice. Wash each grapefruit and dry with a clean cloth. Use a special grapefruit knife for cutting the segments.

grapefruit
Barbados sugar
margarine

Cut off a slice at the top and bottom unless serving in rounded bowls. (This prevents wobble!) Cut in half with a vegetable knife, through the middle, horizontally. Use the grapefruit knife to loosen the flesh all the way round. Also cut between the segments. If you have picked really good fruit, the juice should be running in all directions by now. Place in the grill pan and sprinkle with brown sugar. Dot with margarine and grill gently until the tops begin to brown. Serve immediately with teaspoons and paper serviettes.

Very light – a good appetizer. Serve hot.

Quiche

This is most often served as a main course, but it makes a tasty starter. Serve only a small wedge per person and aim for light, crisp pastry. Recipes are for a seven-inch quiche dish.

Preheat oven at 425-450°F/218-232°C (Gas Mark 7).

Pastry

4 oz (100g) plain 100 per cent wholewheat flour
2 oz (50g) wholewheat self-raising flour
3 oz (75g) soft margarine
about 2 tablespoonsful cold water

Put the flours into a large bowl with the margarine. First blend with a fork and then rub in with the fingers until the mixture resembles fine bread crumbs. Bind with the water then knead to form one ball. (Do not knead too much or the pastry will be tough.) Gently roll out using more wholemeal flour, rolling in one direction only.

Lift half the pastry and slip the rolling pin underneath it. Lift, using the rolling pin, onto the quiche dish, pulling it out carefully so as not to break the pastry. Use the knuckle of one forefinger to press the pastry gently into the bottom edge. Use the fingers to press it to the sides. Cut off excess dough around the top edge, using a sharp knife dipped in flour. Press and pull the top edge of the pastry slightly out over the rim of the dish. Prick the bottom lightly with a fork to release air during baking.

Place the lined quiche dish on a baking sheet and put into the preheated oven, above centre. Bake for ten minutes. Take out of the oven still on the baking sheet.

While you are waiting for the pastry case to bake, get the filling ready. Choose one from the next page.

Mushroom Filling

2 eggs
½ pint (275ml) milk
¼ lb (100g) mushrooms, washed, sliced and lightly fried in
1 tablespoonful of oil

Cheese and Tomato Filling

2 eggs
½ pint (275ml) milk
2 medium tomatoes, sliced
4 oz (100g) grated cheddar cheese

Onion Filling

2 eggs
½ pint (275ml) milk
2 medium onions, peeled, sliced and fried until transparent

In each case the method is the same. Lightly whisk the eggs and milk. Pour into the baked flan case. Add the rest of the filling, distributing evenly. Sprinkle the chives or parsley over the top. Put carefully back into the oven at a lower temperature 375°F/191°C (Gas Mark 5) for 30-35 minutes. Serve hot or cold, cut into wedges.

Note. For a lighter quiche use dried milk reconstituted at double the amount given. This cuts down the fat considerably and makes it less filling. (Add seasoning at the table as some people prefer quiche without it.)

Filling. Serve hot.

Baked Eggs

Small ovenproof 'Cocottes' or ramekins are needed for this dish. Allow one egg per person, preferably brown-shelled and free-range.

Liberally grease each cocotte with margarine and put on a baking sheet in a preheated oven 375°F/191°C (Gas Mark 5) on the middle shelf. After four or five minutes the cocottes will be warm enough. Take out of the oven and break an egg into each one. Put back into the oven for ten to twelve minutes for the eggs to set. Serve as soon as they are ready, with wholemeal bread and margarine or butter. If preferred, serve with hot toast. Put the cocotte on a saucer, with a teaspoon, to serve.

Fairly filling. Serve hot.

HOT VEGETABLE STARTERS

A maddeningly simple starter if the vegetables are *exceptionally good*. Always serve on hot plates with a *dot* (not a knob) of margarine or butter melting on the top. You must get this kind of starter straight from the saucepan, onto hot plates and served at the table without delay. Put seasoning on the table – sea salt and a pepper mill for black peppercorns.

Sprouts

Allow just six or eight per person. Wash sprouts and cut off outer leaves. Cut a slice off the base of each one and cut a three-quarter-inch deep cross to ensure the base cooks right through. Put the prepared sprouts into a saucepan containing $\frac{1}{4}$ pint (150ml) boiling salted water. Put the lid on and turn down the heat. Cook for about seven to ten minutes. Strain in colander and serve.

Light. Serve hot.

Broccoli/Calabrese

Cut into florets or trim the base of the clumps of florets, cutting into the thick stalk. Cook as for sprouts, but with slightly more water.

Light. Serve hot.

Cauliflower

Wash. Trim off the base of the stalk taking the coarse outer leaves with it. Leave the tenderest leaves attached to the white florets. Cut into about four to eight sections, depending on the size. Cook and serve as for sprouts.

Light. Serve hot.

Leeks

Trim off coarse green tops (very little if they are young). Slice off the root. Slit each leek right through lengthways. Open up the layers and wash carefully under the cold tap. Cut into smaller pieces and cook in the absolute minimum of water (slightly salted). Keep the lid on so they can cook in their own steam. Young leeks need about ten to fifteen minutes. Older ones will need up to twenty-five minutes. Strain in a colander and press with the back of a spoon to get rid of excess water. Serve on hot plates with a dot of margarine or butter. Allow four small leeks or two large per person.

Light. Serve hot.

Runner Beans

Allow ½ lb (225g) beans per person. Wash, trim off top, tail and strings as shown. Slice through at an angle. Cook in boiling salted water which comes only half way up the beans, with the lid on. Strain and serve. If the beans are young and very tender they will need about ten minutes. Older, larger beans need up to twenty minutes. Extract a slice with a fork to see when they are done. They should be slightly firm. Serve hot with a dot of butter or margarine.

Light. Serve hot.

French Beans (Green Beans)

Wash, top and tail. Do not attempt to cut off the strings. Use only young tender beans. Cut into two-inch pieces and cook as for runner beans. They will need only seven to ten minutes. Serve with a dot of margarine or butter.

Light. Serve hot.

String Beans

Wash, in a large bowl of water. Pick them over, top and tail. Cook whole in half an inch of boiling salted water for seven to ten minutes with the lid on until tender but still firm. Serve with a dot of margarine or butter.

Light. Serve hot.

Peas

Allow $\frac{1}{2}$ lb (225g) (peas and pods) per person. Shell the peas and cook in a quarter inch of boiling salted water. Young peas will need only five to eight minutes. Strain and serve immediately. If they take longer to cook than this they are not really worth serving on their own as a starter. Top with a dot of margarine or butter.

Fairly filling. Serve hot.

Mangetout Peas

Before the actual peas start to swell in the pod, the pea pods are still tender enough to eat. For each person allow $\frac{1}{4}$ lb (100g) mangetout. Wash them and cut off the tops and tails. Put into a generous amount of boiling salted water and cook with the lid on for six to eight minutes. They should be tender but still firm. Strain and return to the hot pan. Put in a knob of margarine or butter. Toss to melt. Serve immediately with a knife and fork.

Fairly filling. Serve hot.

Baby Beetroot

Choose the very smallest, first of the crop. They should be of similar size. Cut off the leaves and stalk leaving just half an inch still attached to the beet. Leave on the long root at the bottom. Wash off any dirt. Put into boiling, salted water and put the lid on, allowing a space for the steam to escape. (This stops them boiling over.) About half an hour should be enough. Drain in a colander and allow to cool slightly before peeling off the skins. (Wear rubber gloves for this!) Serve hot with a knife and fork.

Fairly filling. Serve hot.

Baby Carrots

These are sometimes called 'finger carrots'. Buy with the green still on and allow about seven per person. Trim off stalks and long top root. Wash. Cook in a quarter of an inch of boiling salted water with the lid on for about seven to ten minutes. Serve sprinkled with freshly chopped parsley.

Fairly filling. Serve hot.

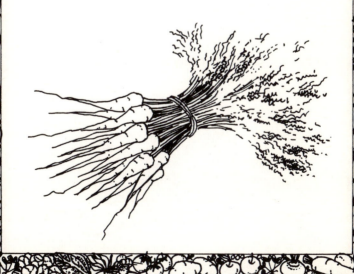

Courgettes (Baby Marrows)

Choose young, tender marrows, allowing one or two per person, depending on size. Wash and trim off stalk part. Slice thinly into rounds. Melt a knob of margarine in a small saucepan and put in the slices. Turn over with a wooden spoon while cooking for three minutes. Season and serve hot. Also good served sprinkled with Parmesan cheese.

Light. Serve hot.

Cheese Sauce

1 oz (25g) margarine
1 oz (25g) 100 per cent wholewheat flour
½ pint (275ml) milk (made with dried milk)
Sea salt and freshly ground pepper
3 oz (75g) cheddar cheese

Melt the margarine in a saucepan. Add the flour and stir well while it cooks for two or three minutes (without turning brown). (Use a wooden spoon.) Gradually blend in the flour a little at a time. When all the milk is used, bring to the boil and then lower heat and stir well. Add the cheese, finely grated and just let it melt into the sauce. Taste and season.

Filling. Serve hot on hot vegetables.

Leeks in Cheese Sauce

Cook the leeks as directed in the hot vegetable section. Serve in a hot dish with cheese sauce (see recipe) poured over. Serve with wholewheat bread and margarine or butter.

Filling. Serve hot.

Spinach with Cheese Sauce

Cook spinach (see p. 65) allowing ½ lb (225g) raw spinach per person. Serve (in a small dish) covered with a layer of cheese sauce. Make sure the spinach is really well drained or the dish will be spoiled by a puddle of pale green water.

Fairly filling. Serve hot.

Index